MONTESSORI
AND
MINDFULNESS

ADAPTATION OF THE 2017 PRESENTATION
AT THE AMI INTERNATIONAL CONGRESS
IN PRAGUE, CZECH REPUBLIC

Susan Mayclin Stephenson

II

OTHER BOOKS IN THIS SERIES

The Joyful Child: Montessori, Global Wisdom for Birth to Three

Child of the World: Montessori, Global Education for Age 3-12+

The Red Corolla, Montessori Cosmic Education (for age 3-6)

The Universal Child Guided by Nature: Adaptation of the 2013 International Montessori Congress Presentation

Montessori and Mindfulness

No Checkmate: Montessori Chess Lessons for Age 3-90+

Montessori Homeschooling, One Family's Story

Aid to Life, Montessori Beyond the Classroom

Please Help Me Do It Myself, Observation and Recordkeeping for the Montessori Primary and Elementary Class

MONTESSORI AND MINDFULNESS

Michael Olaf Montessori Publishers
Arcata, California
www.michaelolaf.net
michaelolafcompany@gmail.com

For translation and foreign publishing rights contact:
michaelolafbooks@gmail.com

ISBN 978-1-879264-19-9

Cover:
From an oil painting "Dancing to the Music" by the author.

When the children had completed an absorbing bit of work, they appeared rested and deeply pleased. It almost seemed as if a road had opened up within their souls that led to all their latent powers, revealing the better part of themselves. They exhibited a great affability to everyone, put themselves out to help others and seemed full of good will.

It was clear to me that the concept of order and the development of character, of the intellectual and emotional life, must derive from this veiled source. Thereafter, I set out to find experimental objects that would make this concentration possible, and carefully worked out an environment that would present the most favorable external conditions for this concentration.

And that is how my method began.

—**Maria Montessori,** *The Child in the Family*

TABLE OF CONTENTS

APPENDIX

MINDFULNESS

What is Mindfulness and what does it have to do with Montessori philosophy or practice? A relatively new concept in the West refers to something that has been explored for centuries in the East. Google *mindfulness* and you will find hundreds of pages of advice for learning to be in the moment, something to help make our fast-paced sometimes hectic lives more manageable, more enjoyable. Most of us are interested in mindfulness because we seem to be always focused on the future, never quite caught up. We want a break.

Most definitions of mindfulness include being deeply involved with, or concentrating on, what we are doing or thinking about in the present moment, without being distracted by what is going on around us or our thoughts about anything but what we are experiencing right now.

The practice of mindfulness in the development of children existed even in Dr. Montessori's work in the San Lorenzo slums of Rome in the beginning of the 20th century. And in our Montessori classrooms we witness it daily when we see a child concentrating deeply on an activity that is just right for his stage of development, an activity that he has chosen for himself, and for which the steps have been made clear. Respecting this activity of the child, protecting it from interruption, is the most important element of Montessori philosophy, at home and in school, at all ages.

Every evening the teacher in this Infant Community in Sweden measures and sets out the flour, yeast, sugar, to make ready for bread baking each morning. In this picture we see a girl of 2 years who has donned the baker's apron and hat, mixed and kneaded the dough, and is cutting it into pieces to bake in a muffin tin to share with her IC friends for lunch. This work done with mindfulness not only meets her needs but also provides a way for her to give to her friends.

Yes there is more to mindfulness than just satisfying the needs of an individual. A great Tibetan teacher whom I met in Dharamsala, India in 2002 defined it this way in a recent talk in Toronto:

It is indeed true that mindfulness is about being aware of oneself, one's thoughts and emotions and actions, but this is not all that it is. Mindfulness means also being aware of others, of the environment, and one's relationship with others and the environment.

He is saying that the practice of mindfulness is not just for ourselves, but it also brings out the best of a person, it helps us to feel part of a community and to define our role in it. It brings about happiness while it spills over as compassion and care for others.

Doesn't this sound like Montessori? Every day we think about these things, not only for ourselves as teachers and parents, but how to best help children develop their own natural tendencies to relate to others and their environment with respect and love. We understand that in Montessori practice we have the secret of giving the experience of mindfulness to children, but what about us?

What would you be thinking about if you were able to watch the video of this little girl baking bread? No matter how many times I watch the video from which this picture was taken, and other video clips of our Montessori children working, I am in the present moment, I am being mindful. Each time I see something new, different, because I have changed. The more we learn about human development the more we see and the more we are. As Montessori parents and teachers we have been given a great gift of spending time each day practicing mindfulness while we are observing and learning from our children.

There are other ways that we can learn to be mindful, to be in the moment. One of these is meditation.

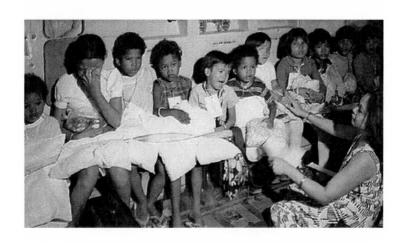

MEDITATION AS A PATH
TO MINDFULNESS

I want to start with a personal story of how I discovered meditation and what it has meant to me. As a college sophomore I traveled for 4 months through Europe, the Middle East, and Asia on the first Semester at Sea, a university on board a ship. The required courses were Current Events in Europe, and Current Events in Asia. Having always been interested in watching people, in human nature, and in questions about why some people are happy and kind and others are not, I signed up for these three courses, as electives, that I thought would teach me about people. I studied The Structure of the Family, Living World Religions, and Comparative Art and Architecture. We attended lectures, studied from morning to night when at sea, and through arranged field trips when we were on land in 22 ports as we circumnavigated the world.

On this trip I visited hospitals, schools, temples, orphanages, slums, universities, and palaces. We had an audience with the Pope and met with Jacques Cousteau and the Prime Minister of Malaysia. I passed out food to the "boat people" in the Hong Kong harbor, many of whom had never left the small crafts they lived on. In Vietnam we met with Vietnamese students and American Special Forces in Saigon (now Ho Chi Minh City). We were the last non-military ship to be allowed into the country and were shot at from the banks of the Saigon River as we sailed to the Mekong Delta during the war. I came home enlightened but also confused and distraught at what I had seen of the disparity of rich and poor, the violence and poverty, and I had seen first hand that there was often more joy and kindness in the lives of the poor than the rich. I wanted to know why, to learn more and to find a way to help bring peace to our world. The anti-war movement of the 1960s gave me a way to be helpful, but discovering Montessori when our first child began to attend a Montessori school in San Francisco offered more powerful potential in this search.

Several years later, taking my first AMI Montessori course, in London, I could see through what I was learning that this was just what I had been looking for. I began to feel empowered with information and tools to be a helpful person, to bring out the very best in the human being from the early years. But I could not let go of what I had seen during my travels. I was impatient.

One day I asked Hilla Patel, my trainer and later director of AMI, the Association Montessori Internationale, how I was going to be able to focus on my students when there was still so much suffering in the world, when there were so many people who needed help.

I said, "Do I wear blinders?"

Her reply was, "No, you learn to meditate." And she introduced me to meditation in London. So that was the beginning. I learned through TM, Transcendental Meditation, to be in the moment, to focus on what was happening now. I could still learn from the past and make plans for the future, but I was effective, and even peaceful and happy, in the present.

This is the class picture in my first elementary, age 6-13, class in 1978, in Saint Croix, US Virgin Islands. We covered the academic work as we spent time in nature, danced, and made music.

Over the years of teaching children from age 2 to 17, I have almost never entered a Montessori environment without having meditated. This has helped me begin each day in peace, to see each child fresh with no pre-conceived expectations, kept me in the moment, and I am sure I have been a better teacher as a result.

In this book I am sharing with you just a little of some of the things I have experienced and have been thinking about over the last almost 50 years about meditation, mindfulness and Montessori. But I do not profess to have all the answers. I will never stop learning about this. There is a lot of research today on the benefits of meditation but I would like to mention several people who I have been following.

Jon Kabat-Zinn is Professor of Medicine Emeritus and creator of the Stress Reduction Clinic and the Center for Mindfulness in Medicine, Health Care, and Society at the University of Massachusetts Medical School. He was also a student **of** Buddhist teachers such **as** Thich Nhat Hanh.

He tells us that the brain can adapt, heal, and renew itself after trauma, compensate for disabilities, rewire itself to overcome dyslexia, and break cycles of depression and obsessive compulsive disorder (OCD). He says that scientists are learning from studies performed on Buddhist monks that it is not only the outside world that can change the brain, so can the mind, and, in particular, focused attention through the practice of mindfulness.

As Dr. Montessori said in addressing the National Education Association, Oakland, California, in 1915 (from A Montessori Journey: 1907-2017, NAMTA)

When you have solved the problem of attention of the child, you have solved the entire problem of education.

Since Dr. Kabat-Zinn began this work, thousands of studies have documented the physical and mental health benefits of mindfulness meditation, inspiring countless programs to adapt this model for schools, prisons, hospitals, veterans' centers, and beyond.

Dr. Richard Davidson is another person I have learned from. He is a professor of psychology and psychiatry at the University of Wisconsin, as well as founder and chair of the Center for Investigating Healthy Minds at the Waisman Center at this university. He is well known for his research in the Neurological effects of meditation. He is breaking ground on relieving posttraumatic stress disorder (PTSD) in returning soldiers through meditation and breathing.

But both of these scientists realize that they are at the beginning of this path of learning. Dr. Davidson says about the brain:

We actually have no idea of how conscious experience arises from this blob of matter that weighs

three pounds. It's really still very much a mystery.
The brain is the most complicated organ in the

universe. We've only taken the first very, very small
baby steps. We're just beginning this journey.

In the mid 1990s AOL, or American Online, was the only way to access the Internet. I think there were not many people online back then because there were chat sessions with famous people where we could ask questions and get a direct answer. One day I saw that the Dalai Lama was going to be in a chat room for 15 minutes. I was ready.

Just before the second hand approached 12:00 noon, I sent in my question:

"At what age is a child ready for seated meditation?" I think someone must have been showing him the procedure ahead of time because the answer came almost immediately. He said, "Only when the child is ready, but not too early."

Since that time I have asked a lot of practitioners and teachers of meditative traditions this question. What

I have learned is that in the Buddhist tradition seated meditation is not taught until the teenage years. I have learned that being able to teach young children meditation, or yoga, takes many years. In fact American Yoga Association (AYA) president Alice Christensen, believes that yoga is not appropriate for children under sixteen because the effect of yoga on nervous and glandular systems may interfere with natural growth.

Dr. Angeline Lillard is Professor of Psychology at the University of Virginia, and author of the most scientifically grounded study of Montessori to date, *Montessori, The Science Behind the Genius.* She says in her paper "Mindfulness Practices in Education: Montessori's Approach" which is quoted extensively at the end of this book:

> *How to implement mindfulness practices with young children is not yet clear; some meditation practices like sitting still for long periods with internally self-regulated focused attention seem developmentally inappropriate. Montessori schooling is a 100-year-old system that naturally incorporates practices that align with mindfulness and are suited to very young children.*

I agree that requiring a child to sit still before age 7 is not appropriate. And even with older children we must be careful about what we require because each child is unique in his development and his mental and physical needs.

In 2005 I visited a non-Montessori country school in Eastern Thailand. When I talked to parents about their daily lives I learned that seated meditation is something that families have always done together in the evenings. But children join in voluntarily and are not required to sit still for any length of time.

The elementary-aged children in this picture are used to this ancient practice of meditation to begin the day where they focus on the teachings of Buddha and remind themselves to care for each other and to follow all of the precepts of their religion appropriate to their age. The session is very short and part of the culture.

Weaving on a loom is a traditional craft in Bhutan so it is natural for it to be an activity in a Montessori class.

This is the kind of spontaneous meditation we see in Montessori. The child choses the activity after being carefully shown how to do the work. She decides how long to work and when it is time to move on to something else. Here are two Montessori students in 3-6 classes in Bhutan.

The child on the left is weaving and the little boy is unrolling a floor mat, which will mark his workspace and protect his work from interruption by others as he concentrates. He will bring the materials that he chooses to the mat, work for a self-directed length of time, and put the material away when he is finished.

Children have their own inner guide that tells them when to move, how to move, when to sit still. Our role is to discover what will inspire each child to act, to move in such a way that is in sync with his stage of development, and allow him to be guided by his own inner wisdom. This is Montessori mindful meditation. In the next chapter, Montessori as a Path to Mindfulness, there will be more examples of just how Montessori supports this inner wisdom, in homes and in the classroom, from the beginning of life.

MONTESSORI AND MINDFULNESS
FROM THE BEGINNING OF LIFE

THE 4 PLANES OF DEVELOPMENT
THE "BULB"

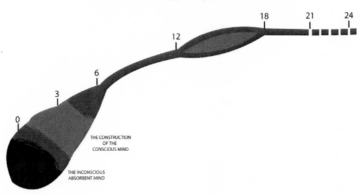

This is a simplified version of Dr. Montessori's "bulb"
from the AMI 0-3 or Assistants to Infancy program
which shows that the construction of the mind
begins before birth.

Human beings have wisdom even before they
are born as they experience their world
sensorially and as they sleep, wake, and move, according
to their needs. In Montessori philosophy, based on years
of observation, human development can be divided into
four distinct phases or planes: 0-6, 6-12, 12-18, 18-24. It is
clear from the illustration that the first plane, prenatal to
age 6, is the greatest period of development, where the
most mental and physical development takes place, and

where our support and understanding are greatly needed.

In the AMI Assistants to Infancy Program (birth to three years), we learn many ways to recognize and respect the child's inner wisdom as a guide to development. We learn to watch for and observe what the child is focusing his attention on, to respect and not interrupt these periods of mindfulness.

Respiratory Autogenic Training, sometimes known as RAT, which was first developed by the obstetrician Umberto Piscicelli in Italy, teaches one to relax, to breathe as in sleeping, even during labor contractions. This is a valuable skill and it takes practice to learn how to do it. Twice a day in most AMI 0-3 teacher training courses, this kind of meditation is practiced in a darkened room as a group. First the words are heard, "We find a comfortable position" and then "We are one with our breathing" and so on. By the time the music begins each of us is quiet in body and mind and completely in the moment.

This training teaches graduates of the course, through personal experience, to be able to prepare families for birth by teaching the body to completely relax between birthing contractions, thus providing the best possible experience for both mother and child.

It also helps the students who are taking the AMI 0-3 course, which is very demanding, to succeed in the work and it has been reported that it also creates a very supportive group. This seems to be another example of the experience of inner peace leading to caring for others.

In the winter between my two-summer A to I training in Denver, I was fortunate to be able to visit the Cristo Re hospital in Rome, Italy where RAT training was being used to prepare women for childbirth. There were two women, both in labor with their first child, and both having taken the RAT training. As a contraction began, they stopped talking or moving and seemed to go into a deep meditative state. Neither of them was feeling the pain we think of as normal during a contraction. It seems that they were so relaxed that the muscles relaxed and stretched. As I visited with the women, the medical person periodically checked the dilation of the cervix. One of them approached 10 cm dilation, which means she was ready to give birth. Just as she stood up to walk into the delivery room, she was surprised to be feeling pain! Within 20 minutes her baby was born.

In my opinion I had observed a miraculous birth and proof of what a trained mind can do to affect the whole body. The following summer when I returned to Denver to complete my A to I training, I was even more aware of the value of RAT twice a day – lying comfortably on the floor in a warm and darkened room, listening to a few words giving relaxation direction and then a recording of "The Adagio in G Minor" by Tomaso Albinoni.

During that same time in Rome I was having lunch

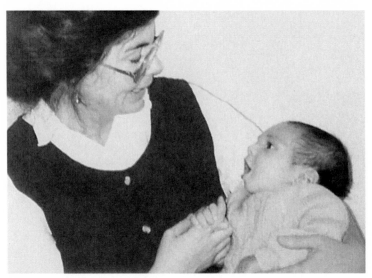

at the home of Dr. Silvana Montanaro, then Head of the AMI Assistants to Infancy training, and holding her new grandson, Raoul, in my arms. He was watching my mouth but as I turned away from him to say something to another person, Dr. Montanaro spoke to me quite firmly. She was adamant that I NOT look away from Raoul until after he looked away from me.

Her advice was life-changing for me and since that time I have had many experiences of respecting eye-contact with infants, allowing them to be the one to end this visual communication. When infants, who I have never met before, notice that I am returning their gaze,

stare for a long time into my eyes. This is mindfulness for both of us and it often feels like a spiritual experience.

Now I am always on the lookout for young children watching and learning. Here is an example of the interest a young child has for watching the face of his mother as she is eating. His eyes followed every detail as she placed the food in her mouth and then chewed it. He smiled as though he were witnessing one of the most amazing performances in his life so far. This shows the

tendency of the very young to be in the moment, aware of surroundings, and fascinated by the activities of the family.

The easily transported *ger* or *yurt* is the home of the nomadic families of Mongolia as they follow the herds of yak, camels, goats, sheep, and horses from one grazing spot to another.

A few years ago I was invited to give a talk in Mongolia. As always I wanted to learn as much as I could about the traditional practices of raising children in this country. My hosts arranged for me to travel into the countryside to visit a nomad family.

Inside of this herder home there is no child's room or floor bed, but rather two or three single beds that serve as sofas during the day arranged around the cooking and heating stove in the middle. There is a place for a container of water, a small table with stools, artwork, and a Buddhist altar reflecting the religion of most of Mongolia.

You can see that the infant has room to explore on a beds but that he is fastened to the wall by a cord so he will not fall onto the floor and find himself near the stove. During our visit the older boy went in and out of the door as he pleased. The children grow up with a great deal of freedom to be outside in the fresh air.

I was very welcome to ask questions about the lives of children in the Mongolian herder society. The mother, a high school science teacher, and her husband, have decided to live the nomad life while their children are young. They feel that this is a healthier way to live than in the city and they have good memories of their own early years living a peaceful life close to nature and solitude. She had not heard of Montessori but when she found that Dr. Montessori was also a scientist she became more interested in learning during our visit.

During our conversation at one point I looked over

at her infant who was reaching for a piece of dried yak cheese that had been placed in front of him. I pointed out the intense concentration of the infant, how he used his

whole body in reaching, and the details of how he used his fingers, thumbs, and hands. I talked about the myelination process in developing voluntary muscles of the body and how movement improves the brain in developing both mental and physical abilities. It became clear that this concentration is an example of mindfulness. Mindfulness of the child as he experimented with his physical abilities and mindfulness of us adults as we forgot everything we had been thinking about concerning the past and the future and were totally engrossed in our observation of the child.

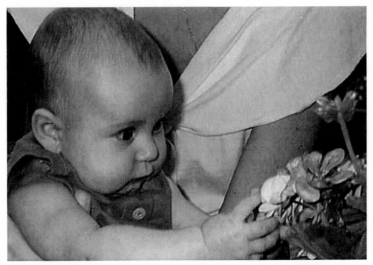

As we were leaving, the mother invited us to return because she wanted to learn more about her children. I am sure that her enthusiasm to learn is one of the reasons that *The Joyful Child: Montessori, Global Wisdom for Birth to Three*, is being translated into the Mongolian Language.

In the beginning of life the child experiences his environment immediately by smell and taste of the mother, and with ears and eyes as he explores visually the fine details of his home.

I sometimes wonder what it must be like to, for so many weeks and months, be able to only SEE a flower or any object and then finally to TOUCH it for the first time. To be able to finally explore the soft and hard

areas, the feel of the corolla, the pistil, the stamens, the calyx, to touch and bend and hold it up to a cheek. The wonder of such an experience is captured in the eyes of the child in this picture who is touching a geranium for the first time.

Concentrated attention as one works on a task is respected in the Montessori environment in the same way. Adults do not interrupt the children, and we teach children how to watch quietly without interrupting a friend's concentration.

The older child in this picture has drawn around the country pieces of the Montessori puzzle map of North and Central America. Then he began to very carefully paint each country with watercolor paints. The young child has already learned that is it fine to watch a friend who is working, but that it is not okay to interrupt his deep concentration.

This picture is taken from a video I took in a Montessori class. In the video we can see that the young child tries to get as close as possible, to see the care with which her friend is painting, without interrupting. And it is clear as we watch several minutes of the video that the older child knows that his work is not going to be interrupted.

We know today from research on mirror neurons that the child who is watching is also learning. In this instance the little girl who is so attentive and focused on observing the actions of the other child is stimulating the same neurons in her own brain as is the child who is painting.

The deep level of concentration that we want to see and protect does not occur with every activity but it depends on many things. In the home for the very young child it is often in the handling of objects that he has seen others handling, doing things that he has seen others do. In the classroom it occurs when the child has been given a lesson on an activity that matches his skill and interest.

During our AMI Montessori teacher training we learn how to observe children carefully so that we know when to offer which activity.

We spend many hours, under the direction of an experienced teacher trainer, practicing giving these lessons to each other so the logical steps of the activity are clear and precise and the lesson to the child will entice him to want to do the work. At the end of such a teacher training course, for exams, a trainee is asked to demonstrate a lesson on a specific piece of material, to discuss fully all of the steps or stages of that activity, its purpose, the average age of the child for that lesson, what activities were necessary to prepare the child for this one, what language is connected to the material, what other activities in the classroom are at a similar level of development, and how all of this practical work connects with the deep theory of Montessori. With this kind of training the teacher is prepared to be in the moment and to observe and meet the child's needs by offering the kind of activity he is ready to concentrate on and master.

The choice of materials and activities in a Montessori class is not random. The kind of deep concentration that is valuable only occurs during certain

kinds of activities and with certain materials. And we now have over 100 years of valuable experience that show us just what materials and which lessons, which have been tested all over the world, lead to such concentration for the child.

As Dr. Montessori first began to observe the positive changes brought about in children as the result of deep levels of concentration she began to search for just which materials and activities brought out the results that were considered so remarkable, she said in the book *The Child in the Family*:

I took what happened to the children to be the law, and this made it possible for me to resolve completely the problem of education. It was clear to me that the concept of order and the development of character, of the intellectual and emotional life, must derive from this veiled source. Thereafter, I set out to find experimental objects that would make this concentration possible, and carefully worked out an environment that would present the most favorable external conditions for this concentration. And that is how my method began.

In the next chapters we look at our Montessori practice today. There are ways that we help and there are ways that we get in the way of mindfulness or concentration. There are many, many examples of focus, attention, mindfulness, happiness, and compassion in our classes each day.

MINDFULNESS, SUPPORT AND IMPEDIMENTS

Support of Mindfulness and Concentration

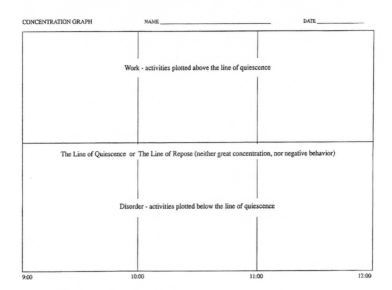

CONCENTRATION GRAPH   NAME _____   DATE _____

Work - activities plotted above the line of quiescence

The Line of Quiescence or The Line of Repose (neither great concentration, nor negative behavior)

Disorder - activities plotted below the line of quiescence

9:00   10:00   11:00   12:00

There are many ways that we support mindfulness and concentration in our classrooms, but there are also things that we do that can prevent the deep concentration that is the most important part of a child's experience. In the chapter "My Contribution to Experimental Science", in *The Advanced Montessori method, Volume 1*, Dr. Montessori gave us one of the most important tools we have.

She called these graphs, such as the one pictured here, "work curves" because they help us visualize the way a child works in the Montessori class. This example graph covers three hours from 9:00 to 12:00. In my school the arrival time for children was between 8:30 and 9:00 in the morning so we could be quite sure that the 3-hour work period was at least 3 hours long.

In the middle you see what Dr. Montessori called the "line of quiescence" or sometimes called the "line of repose" which indicates that the child is not really involved with a positive activity but neither is he interrupting anyone else or causing any kind of a disturbance. The level of involvement or concentration of the child's "work" is plotted above that line. The deeper the concentration, the higher the line. And any "disorder' is plotted below the line.

Some Montessori teachers track a child's concentration by recording notes during this period in a linear way, recording the time and the activity and the level of concentration, and then plotting this information on the graph later in the day. I probably did that in the beginning but mostly I remember plotting the child's activity and level of concentration in a morning directly on the graph.

When I was teaching primary (age 2-6) and elementary (age 6-12+) classes I kept a clipboard on the top of a bookcase (I have never had a desk no matter what age my students) along with my weeklong plan of suggested lessons for each child. I plotted a work curve of concentration for one child each day. Eventually I began calling them "concentration graphs" because over time they show an increase in a child's level of concentration. They were the most impressive observation tools that I had to share with parents in meetings with a family. The use of these graphs helped parents understand the value we put on this, and enabled them to look for examples in the home.

This and the other graphs I use in this chapter are taken directly from Dr. Montessori's book so I urge you to go to them and learn more. Here is a graph of a new child. Dr. Montessori described this graph of one of "The Curve of Work of a Very Poor Child almost Entirely

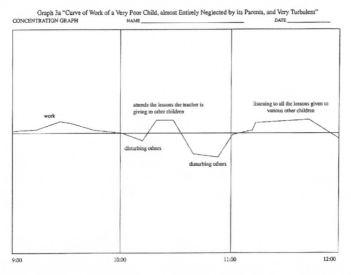

Graph 3a "Curve of Work of a Very Poor Child, almost Entirely Neglected by its Parents, and Very Turbulent"

Neglected by Its Parents and Very Turbulent." It is clear

that he is spending a lot of time with the teacher, perhaps as he learns how the class functions, and because he has not yet discovered the joy of concentration he at times disturbs others. It is quite common for a teacher to invite a new child to accompany her as she gives lessons to others rather than requiring the non-Montessori "time-out" way of distracting a child. In this way rather than separating and embarrassing a child she helps him feel included and she can see what attracts his attention as she makes plans to invite him to his own individual lessons on the path to concentration.

This could be the concentration graph of the whole class, not just one child. As when a new class is beginning, or when school begins for the year, we often

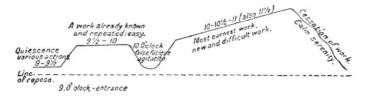

When this work ceases, the children are gentle, calm and happy.

see what is called "false fatigue". That means that just as with this graph children seem to choose easy work in the beginning of the morning, and then somewhere is the middle of the morning there is a period of agitation. If the teacher knows what is happening she will sit down and wait. For this is not real fatigue rather it is a time when a child might be taking a deep breath and thinking to himself, "Okay, I have done the easy work to warm up, now what do I want to tackle this morning to make some real progress? What will be my great work of the morning?"

After the period of false fatigue often comes what is called the "great work of the morning" or the work that challenges the child to grow and requires him to concentrate deeply. The teacher who does not know that this is "false fatigue" might call the children together for a group activity. This is a shame because then none of the children will experience the great work.

Sometimes during the first days and weeks for a new child we could expect to see 10 or more different very short activities in 3 hours. These are things he has begun to explore but are not repeated and have not yet called for deep concentration. In this graph the child is only doing two things in the morning and so, even though he is still having times when the line goes into the bottom half of the graph, the concentration length of time and level is rising.

These lessons, exact and fascinating, given in an intimate way to each child separately, are the teacher's offering to the depths of the child's soul. Then, one day, one of these tiny spirits will awaken, the inner "self" of some child will go out to an object which it will temporarily possess, his attention will focus on the repetition of an exercise the doing of which brings increased skill, and the child's radiant

*and contented manner will show that his spirit has
been reborn.*

— **Montessori, The Absorbent Mind**

Advance towards Order

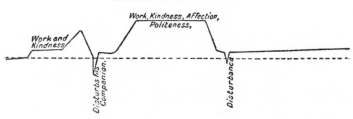

Dr. Montessori called this work curve "Advance Toward Order" because, even though on this day the child is not exhibiting deep concentration on a specific activity, and even though he disrupts working companions twice, he is exhibiting kindness, affection, and politeness to others. This kind of improvement of personality is something we see all the time in our classes as a child begins to concentrate. As a child is offered an activity or work that is just right for him and is given a careful lesson as to how to do the activity, as he becomes engaged with it and begins to concentrate deeply, he becomes a better, kinder, more polite, and happier human being.

Impediments to Mindfulness and Concentration

Sometimes there are impediments to concentration that cannot be helped. For example in places where there is not yet real understanding of Montessori the adult to student radio causes problems. Dr. Montessori recommended one teacher and one non-teaching assistant to 30+ children. Of course this only works when the teachers is very well trained.

Another impediment can be state or country required whole group outside play or group snack or scheduled group naps. These are frustrating and the only solution is to work with the present authorities to explain how Montessori works. Explaining the importance of concentration and the 3-hour work period is a good place to start.

But there are two main impediments that we can do something about to support mindful concentration in our classes. The first is to be sure we schedule at least 3-hours of child-choice, uninterrupted work time each morning, 5 days a week. The second it to be sure that the materials in the classroom are those that have been tested for over 100 years all over the world to inspire deep concentration and to eliminate the "supplementary" materials that have no real purpose, scatter the child's energy, and do not lead to concentration.

Years ago I was looking closely on the computer screen this picture of a Montessori 3-6 birthday celebration that I had scanned. In this celebration a child circles a candle that represents the sun as he holds the globe in his hands. Each circling of the candle represents

one year of his life, a concept actually more appropriate for the 6-12 class. As the child completes each cycle the teacher holds up a picture of that year and the children say, "And then he was one." or "And then he was two." and so on.

As I looked at this picture close up I could see for the first time the expressions of complete boredom on the faces of the children who had been pulled away from concentrating on their individual work to "celebrate." I did the math: 30 children x 3 years in the class = 90 birthdays! And all of the children were required to attend and to celebrate each and every birthday. No wonder they were bored.

Seeing these faces brought home to me the reason why, except in a few instances when group activities are useful and necessary, we do not have required whole-group activities in AMI Montessori. These exceptions might be the beginning of a new class, or bringing in a few new children to an established class. Or the teacher might invite 3-4 children who don't know what to do to join her in a story or manners lesson. There may be other times when gathering all of the children together is important, but it should never be a regularly scheduled "lesson" during the 3-hour work period. There are no "required" group or collective lessons, no regular "circle"

time, in authentic Montessori classes.

Here are some close-up pictures of the children who were required, rather than being invited, to attend this group birthday celebration. I suggest that it is fine to have this birthday celebration and for the birthday child to invite a few of his friend to watch him walk the years. This is what I did in my classes. It was lovely to hear children from the far corners of the room, as they worked diligently on their chosen activity, chant along with the others, "And then he was one."

As Dr. Montessori says about the giving of lessons in a Montessori class, in the book *Creative Development in the Child, the Montessori Approach, Volume II*:

> *This presentation is given, not to a group of children, but individually, to help the child to grow mentally. We prepare this special environment to help his growth, to offer him freedom so that he can proceed with his work in a normal way. The collective lessons are given only to the child who has not yet been normalized. After normalization each child grows individually, in his own way. One child may be ready for the lesson one day and another child another day. . . . If we give a lesson we do not command all the children to stop what they are doing in order to listen. Many children may have absolutely no interest in the lesson and we may bore them.*

Recently I saw the same thing a school in South American where I consulted. I do not mean to criticize the teacher as she was doing her best to reach, instruct, excite each of the children with an interesting lesson on the continents of the world; but it is never possible.

I see these same bored body positions and facial expressions everywhere I work, at all ages, from infant communities to high school classes.

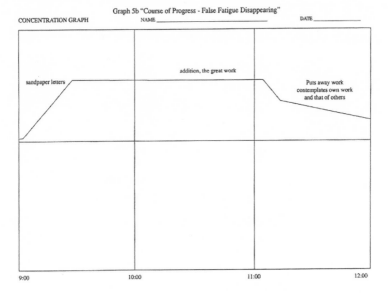

Graph 5b "Course of Progress - False Fatigue Disappearing"

CONCENTRATION GRAPH   NAME _____   DATE _____

sandpaper letters

addition, the great work

Puts away work
contemplates own work
and that of others

9:00   10:00   11:00   12:00

Here is another of Dr. Montessori's graphs. In this one there is no false fatigue. This child works steadily throughout the 3-hour work period. And not on a long list of easy tasks which we sometimes see when the child just picks anything to look busy and not because it calls to him

Think about it. If we have arrived at a stage where most of the children are functioning at a high level of concentration as shown in the graph, it would be against everything we believe in to interrupt this for a required group lesson. In the 6-12+ classes, there are 5 scheduled great lessons given in the beginning of the year – but even then children are invited – not required to attend. Our goal at any age is the kind of child-guided period of concentration that we see in this graph.

Notice the end of the line in this graph where Dr. Montessori records, "Puts away work. Contemplates own work and that of others."

As we will see later in this book, a lot of creative work occurs when the body is still and the mind is working. When we see a child watching another and not interrupting, or just sitting and thinking, this can be very important "work" which can lead to satisfaction and kindness if it is not interrupted. This is mindfulness.

> ... *when the cycle is completed, the child*
> *detaches himself from his internal concentration;*
> *refreshed and satisfied, he experiences the higher*
> *social impulses, such as desiring to make confidences*
> *and to hold intimate communion with other souls.*
> — **Montessori** *Advanced Montessori Method Vol I*

There is a lot of evidence to support the value of a child's contemplation in the classroom. We are mistaken in thinking that a child must be constantly doing something with his hands in order to be mindful,

concentrating, or to be using his time in what we would consider a valuable way. Even the greatest minds learned that, in creating a great work, no more than a few hours a day was spent actually "on task" and the rest in contemplation of the work.

Here is one example from an article entitled "A Better Way to Work", that explores the work habits of

Darwin (seen here at age 7), Dickens, Ingmar Bergman, and others. (www.nautil.us):

> *They only spent a few hours a day doing what we would recognize as their most important work. The rest of the time they were hiking mountains, taking naps, going on walks with friends, or just sitting and thinking. Maybe the key to unlocking the*

> *secret of their creativity lies in understanding not just how they labored but how they rested.*

The education of children in Finland has been in the news in the last few years as a success story to watch. It seems that they have learned to value a balance of the highest level of academics and down time. The schools days are shorter and there is no homework.

Just as in Montessori elementary classes each student proceeds at his or her own pace, takes an active role in designing their own work schedules and learning activities, their own individual program in various subjects according to each student's interests. Also like Montessori they form groups to work on projects and the academic areas overlap. The focus is on helping students take increasing responsibility for their own learning, and for developing into complete and happy human beings.

In the recent movie "Where Shall We Invade Next" Michael Moore researches, in his unique style, some of the good social programs in a series of countries. For education innovation he goes to Finland. Here is a transcript of the relevant part of this movie:

Teacher 1, "They do not have homework."

Moore, "Wait, so you reduce the homework you give them at school?"

Teacher 1, "Yes. They should have more time to be kids. To be youngsters. To enjoy the life."

Moore, "So they have no homework. What if all they want to do is climb a tree?"

Teacher 2, "They could climb a tree. They can come climb a tree but they end up while climbing a tree probably finding out about different insects they can come to explore next day and tell me about what they found.

Moore, "Compared to the older kids how many hours a day do the younger ones go to school?"

Teacher 2, "Twenty hours a week."

Moore, "Oh man. Does this three or four hours a week include the lunch hour?"

Teacher 2, "Yes"

Moore, "How are you learning anything? How are you getting anything done?"

Teacher 3, "Your brain has to, it has to relax now and then. If you just constantly work, work, work, then you stop learning and there is no use of doing that for a longer period of time."

Moore, "Finland's students have the shortest school days and the shortest school years in the entire Western world. They do better by going to school less."

Teacher 3, "Here it is so student centered that when we had to redo our playground we had the architects come in and talk to the kids."

Moore, "Were they listened to?"

"Yes there are things on our playground that the students really wanted.

Teacher 4, "We try to teach them to be happy, a happy person and to respect others and respect yourself."

Moore, "You're concerned with their happiness."

Teacher 4, "Oh yes."

Moore, "What the hell do you teach?"

Teacher 4, "I teach math."

Moore, "So the math teachers says, the first thing out of your mouth of what you wanted these students to get out of school was to be happy. Have a happy life."

Teacher 4, "Yep."

Moore, "And you're the math teacher."

Please do not get the idea that these children, and also children in Montessori classes, are just doing whatever they want with no guidance and help from the teachers! In Finland a master's degree is required and teachers are respected and very well paid and they know how to teach. AMI teacher training is at the same graduate school level and, just as Dr. Montessori's did in the very beginning, they are trained to carefully observe each student and to keep exacting notes and records of what each is interested in, and what he needs to make progress physically, emotionally, socially, and academically in each area of the curriculum.

I continually see that teaching this way absolutely supports mindfulness in the teacher. Rather than lesson plans where the traditional teacher knows exactly what she is going to "teach" all day long, the Montessori teacher is constantly observing and adjusting, observing and adjusting, always in the present moment.

The second impediment to concentration that is for the most part under our control is the selection of materials for the classroom. One of the main causes of the lowering of levels of concentration in children in Montessori classes is the addition of non-Montessori materials to the standard collection taught in AMI training courses. Sometimes these materials are called "extension", "transition", or "supplementary" materials, but they are not helpful.

It is quite common, unfortunately, when a teacher is not seeing enough concentration in the classroom, that she adds more materials. This has the opposite effect, wasting the child's time and energy and not leading to concentration. Also, over the years, many people have attempted to "improve" the materials without fully understanding the reasons for their exacting construction.

For over 100 years research has been conducted as to just what materials provide for the opportunity of concentration and mastery in Montessori classes.

Here is information from the AMI website (heeps://ami-global.org/materials) about Montessori materials:

Dr. Montessori, in her initial work in 1907 in San Lorenzo, observed that the younger children were intensely attracted to sensory development apparatus. The children used these materials spontaneously, independently, repeatedly and with deep concentration. They emerged from this spontaneous activity renewed and with a profound sense of inner satisfaction. Montessori method is based on the spontaneous activity of the child which is aroused precisely by the interest the child takes in the material.

From this initial discovery, over many years of observation and trial and error, Dr. Montessori and her son Mario, went on to design an entire range of Montessori materials.

In order for the materials to be of optimum benefit they must be presented to the child at the appropriate stage in his or her development by a trained Montessori teacher. The materials then allow the child to engage in self-directed, purposeful activity. The materials are beautiful and enticing and are displayed in an orderly and accessible way.

All the apparatus must be meticulously in order, beautiful and shiny, in perfect condition. Nothing must be missing, so that to the child it always seems new, complete and ready for use.

Today, the Association Montessori Internationale Material Committee continues to oversee the development and manufacture of the Montessori materials.

Dr. Angeline Lillard who took an AMI course is conducting valuable research on the value of Montessori education. One study shows that children fare better in classrooms with only AMI approved Montessori materials. And another shows that removing the non-Montessori materials from classrooms for a period of 4 months improved students' executive function and reading scores, and had some impact on math as well, relative to children in a classroom that retained non-Montessori materials. See these articles and more at her website (see back of this book)

At the AMI web site you will find a list of the approved Montessori material manufacturers but if you look further you will see links to projects around the world where it would not be possible for teachers to purchase materials from Western manufacturers. One of these is The Corner of Hope, a pilot program that was begun in 2010, located in New Canaan, an IDP (internally displaced person) camp in Kenya, Africa. This is a combination school and AMI training center.

The teachers become sufficiently well trained so that when they leave the camp they can continue to create their own Montessori schools, educational resources and materials from local sources in other places.

Here is a quote about this project from HEA (Humanitarian Education Accelerator) Global Innovations: https://hea.globalinnovationexchange.org

Each teacher makes for themselves a complete set of teaching materials sourced from locally available materials.

In effect, each teacher becomes autonomous and effectively creates 'a school in a box' that releases them from dependence on external agencies supplying teaching equipment. The local making of materials is a profound principle; it sends the message 'I can do it by myself if you will just show me how'. It engages the individual in creating something valuable for the future of the children; it creates the possibility of replicating, mending and replacing when needed. The cost of creating a vibrant and fascinating range of hands on, brain-based scientifically designed developmental materials is negligible given their longevity.

Corner of Hope

The construction of these materials is not left up to chance. It is carefully guided as part of the AMI teacher-training course that certifies these women as teachers. Their materials attract the children, inspire them to precision in action, and the work they perform with their hands brings forth learning through careful attention and deep concentration.

Now I would like to share a different way of looking at the question of mindfulness and Montessori through the very interesting insight of a well-known Montessori speaker and writer, Mihaly Csikszentmihalyi.

FLOW, THE SECRET TO HAPPINESS

Mihály Csikszentmihalyi, a Hungarian psychologist, is noted for his study of what makes life worth living, in happiness and creativity. He is best known for his research on what he calls *flow* which can be described as deep concentration on an activity not because someone has told one to do it, or for any kind of reward or praise, but for its own sake, intrinsically motivated. During the experience of *flow*, time flies, and every action, movement, and thought follows inevitably from the previous one. One's whole being is involved, and one is using one's skills to the utmost. Dr. Csikszentmihalyi's research has shown that people are happiest when they are in the state of *flow*. And this occurs when they are working on something. How did he discover this?

He developed the Experience Sampling Method at the University of Chicago in the early 1970s. Each person participating in the study wore a pager that was programmed to "beep" at random times during the day. When this happened the activity and what the subject was thinking about and where he was were all recorded. This has provided valuable insight into the questions of what makes a person happy. For example, he discovered that such simple activities of gardening, cooking, making music, and even working are very likely to be experienced as *flow*, but passive leisure activities such as watching television or relaxing are not. At least 10,000 people from all over the world have now participated in these studies of *flow*.

Dr. Csikszentmihalyi has been a frequent speaker and writer in the Montessori field because the mental state that is experienced as happiness and creativity is what we observe occurring during deep concentration in our Montessori environments. I would call *flow* an example of mindfulness.

A very good first introduction to Flow can be seen at the TED talk, "Flow, the Secret to Happiness". Here is the beginning of this talk transcribed.

> *I grew up in Europe, and World War II caught me when I was between seven and 10 years old. And I realized how few of the grown-ups that I knew were able to withstand the tragedies that the war visited on them – how few of them could even resemble a*

normal, contented, satisfied, happy life once their job,
their home, their security was destroyed by the war.
So I became interested in understanding what
contributed to a life that was worth living

Here is an example of an experiment with high school students in China. Each student was given a pager programmed to go off at 10 unpredictable times during a school day. Each time the pager sounded, the students were instructed to identify what they were doing, what they were thinking about, and how they are feeling.

The teacher was giving a very interesting and entertaining whole-group lesson on the Genghis Khan. As the students' pagers went off during the lesson this is what the students recorded as their thoughts:

Of 27 students in the class, 25 didn't mention
anything vaguely connected with China; they
mentioned their dates, their coming football game,
how hungry they were, how sleepy they were, etc.
There were 2 who mentioned China but nothing
about the Genghis Khan.

— **"Flow and Education",**
The NAMTA Journal Vol. 22, no. 2, 1997

The
NAMTA
Journal

N · A · M · T · A

Dr. Csikszentmihalyi says that in Montessori schools we are ahead in the area of figuring out what makes life meaningful, in creating the conditions for flow, because children can choose their own work, can concentrate without being interrupted, and they can work on their own at their own speed, and thus progress naturally in improving their skills. There are several valuable articles on flow published in the NAMTA (North American Montessori Teachers Association) journals. And back issues are available through the website: http://www.montessori-namta.org

Dr. Csikszentmihalyi's work on happiness and creativity validates the importance of the Montessori practice of providing a 3-hour work period uninterrupted by group lessons, schedules, and assignments, when a child is free to move from one activity to the next directed from within. For children older than seven years these self-directed, uninterrupted work periods are measured not by hours but by days or weeks. Each child's individual work plan, created at a private meeting with the teacher, is 1-2 weeks in length and through it a student learns to be responsible for completing the state or country standard curriculum work, to follow his interests, to do research, to create group projects, and to manage his time responsibly.

As Dr. Montessori says about these older children:

> *The elementary school period presents itself . . . as a continuation of the 'Children's Houses' . . .. We see a child occupied for seven or eight consecutive days with the same work. Another child becomes interested in the potentialities of the arithmetical frame, and perseveres with the same work for days, until his knowledge of it has matured.*
> **— Montessori, Advanced Montessori Method, Vol I**

Sometimes I make a quick sketch of my day, following the guide of Dr. Montessori's Work Curves or Concentration Graphs in order to explore and document the experience of *flow* in my own life.

On the next page is a concentration graph of a productive, a "good", day at home.

I do not spend all day actually painting or writing, but while I am working at home during the weekdays I also spend some time gardening, cooking, eating lunch, washing dishes, walking and so forth. During these times, my brain is processing and solving problems or puzzles connected to my work. When I go back to painting or writing I can create anew. I think this is what

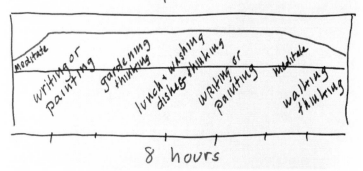

SUSAN - Good DAY - In Flow

meditate writing or painting gardening thinking lunch + washing dishes thinking writing or painting meditate walking thinking

8 hours

a child is experiencing in the uninterrupted 3-hour work period in class as he sometimes works with his hands

and other times he sits and thinks, or observes others working, or he takes a break to walk on the line,

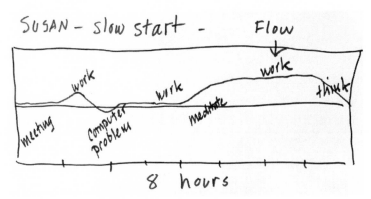

SUSAN - slow start - Flow

work work work think meeting Computer problem meditate

8 hours

and then gets back to work.

Here is a graph of a not so productive day.

When I was in the Montessori classroom I would observe each child as they entered to see if he knew exactly what he wanted to work on first (sometimes waking up in the morning knowing this!), or if he needed to look around a bit for inspiration, or discuss a project with a peer, or if he would be open to a suggestion or a lesson by me. But as I learned in my first AMI 2.5-6 training in London in 1970, I NEVER would schedule an activity first thing in the morning because the goal is to help children get in touch with their own interests and make their own choices of work as they enter the class in the morning. And of course this is not the time for parent/teacher conversations as the teacher is working from the moment the first child enters the room!

However, in my own workday as a writer and artist, if I have any required activity to schedule such as a phone call or a meeting, I schedule it at the beginning of the day to get it over with so the rest of the day will be cleared to concentrate on work. Look at this graph. In the first hour on this day I had a meeting to attend that took all of my attention away from the main creative work of the day. Then I wrote or painted. Then you can see that the line goes below the midline because I was frustrated with a computer problem. Some work was accomplished but not at all as much as in the first chart. And I did not feel as satisfied at the end of the day.

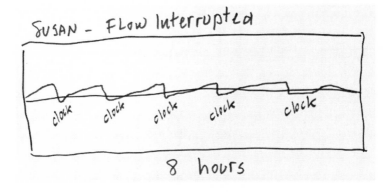

Here is an example of a day of never reaching a high level of concentration. It was an experiment.

During my elementary training it was suggested that if we have a student in a 6-12 class that is frustrated by not getting much work done that we suggest he record just how he spends a day by watching the clock and recording the details of his work and time. This is a remedial activity but sometimes I see it as regular practice in classrooms as a way of record keeping so I tried it just see what it felt like to stop and think about everything I was doing during the day. You can see what happened. As I looked at the clock and recorded the time and the activity, just as children are asked to do, *flow* was completely interrupted and I had lost contact with what my intention was to do next.

Usually as I finish one section of work or restful activity something inside, some intuition toward balance, leads me to the next activity. When I stopped to assess my activities this intuition, the process, was blocked and I never reached the level of concentration or completion of satisfying work that makes me feel at the end of the day that I have really accomplished something.

I discussed this with my friend neuroscientist Adele Diamond who knows a lot about Montessori. I said, "When I finish a task during a work day to look at the clock and record the time, as children are sometimes asked to do, it was like being forced to move to a part of my brain where no real concentration is happening, where connections could not be made, and where nothing was discovered or created.

Her reply? "I agree. You want to be in the moment. Once you are observing yourself being in the moment, you are no longer in the moment."

As she had told us in keynote speech at the Annual General Meeting of The Association Montessori International in Amsterdam in 2010:

> *In order to create, one must be in the moment*
> *and be allowed to stay there.*

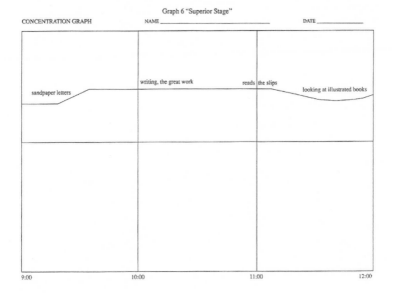

Graph 6 "Superior Stage"

CONCENTRATION GRAPH   NAME _____   DATE _____

sandpaper letters

writing, the great work   reads the slips   looking at illustrated books

9:00   10:00   11:00   12:00

Here is one of my favorites of Dr. Montessori's examples. She calls it the "superior stage" in the development of concentration.

Learning to be mindful is a skill just like any other. It takes practice. This graph is that of a child who has had a lot of experience concentrating and is getting really good at it. Notice that the child enters the room already concentrating! Maybe he thought about something he was doing the day before and could hardly wait to get back to it. This great start of the day carries him through the 3-hour work period deeply concentrating and probably experiencing *flow*. Imagine what would have happened had there been a required group lesson as soon as he arrived.

His first choice was sandpaper letters. Next writing and reading the words he has written, the great work of the morning. And at the end of the morning a period of contemplation, perhaps the brain organizing the previous experience or supplementing it, in preparation for the next work.

It is quite often the case that the teacher also enters the classroom already in *flow*. It is quite exciting to be a Montessori teacher, to know where each child is in each area of study, to have worked with the materials so much that the steps of the lessons are "in our hands" and ready to show to a child, to have a list of possibilities of what to offer each child during the day but to know that by the end of the morning things could have turned out quite differently because she followed each child's unique path through the day. The teacher must be in the moment to work this way.

I found it to be true with students in the classroom, and sometimes even now working at home, that one can be so involved with a project that when going home or even when going to sleep at night one is impatient,

excited and looking forward to the next day to be able to get back to the work. This is *flow*.

As Dr. Csikszentmihalyi says, *flow* can occur for a few hours, a few days, or even longer. It usually involves just one person in the experience, but it can occur when one is working with others as long as everyone is focused on the task at hand. I would like to give two examples. The following are descriptions of *flow* by my own daughters, grown up Montessori students who I believe have learned to balance their lives aided by their experience as Montessori students

Ursula has worked for many years as an environmentalist, a protector of rivers, and a rafting guide. This is a picture of her rafting with her daughter Alexandra. Here is how she describes the *flow* experience of leading a group of people on river trips:

Flow is different in two instances — leading a trip over several days, or running a rapid. In both situations there is complete focus on the moment; there are decisions to be made instantly; there is no thought of oneself, and certainly there is timelessness, being removed from everyday life and time. There is a feeling of ecstasy at the height of running a challenging rapid and when everything is going well for everyone on the trip. When I have led several trips on the same river, there is a chance of boredom setting in unless unpredictable weather or other variables challenge the leaders' skills – "will we get to camp in time, will we get the tents set up before the rain, will the planned food last the trip, etc." – in which case we the leaders must work as a team to make everything work for all. Then again we are in flow.

I like what she said about boredom setting in. Occasionally when I have been working as a school consultant I have heard a teacher say, instead of "Can I help you find something interesting to do?" or "Would you like a lessons on _____?" something like this, "You need to find something to do."

And then I watch the child pick something easy, not interesting or challenging, just to look busy because the teacher is watching. Does this sound familiar? Being a Montessori teacher who supports the kind of concentration that those in *flow* are experiencing means being sure that the activity offered to the child, as Dr. Csikszentmihalyi says, is the child's choice, involves the whole being, and uses his skills to the utmost. He says, "To achieve a *flow* state, a balance must be struck between the challenge of the task and the skill of the performer. If the task is too easy or too difficult, *flow* cannot occur. Both skill level and challenge level must be matched and high; if skill and challenge are low and matched, then apathy results."

Ursula's older sister Narda works in medical clinics in Portland, Oregon. She sometimes volunteers with New York Medics, an organization that brings the best of Western medical practice to the most needy emergency situation in the world. This picture shows her working in 2016 in Iraq. She said in one email home:

American, Lithuanian, Kurdish, French and,
mostly Iraqi volunteers – are extraordinary. Can I

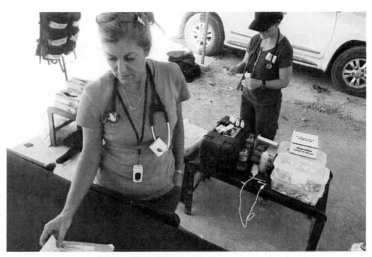

say that I am so very happy to be here? All my years
of training are being fully used and challenged.

After receiving this I emailed her a description from Mihaly Csikszentmihalyi's book *Flow, the Psychology of*

Optimal Experience, on how one surgeon described flow. She said that it is exactly what she was experiencing in Iraq. Here is the quote from the book:

> *The intense focus necessary for surgery blocks out all distractions from the task at hand. This experience, combined with use of one's skills and doing valuable work can be exhilarating. There is immediate feedback of success in the work combined with the possibility of always doing things better, of improving one's skills. But the satisfaction is not just of the individual but includes being part of an event involving a number of additional players. It is exhilarating to be part of a well-trained team functioning smoothly and efficiently.*

I hope this helps us appreciate the incredible gift we give children when we work in our Montessori classrooms. What they are creating now, the habits they are forming will be valuable for the rest of their lives.

Here we see two young children being in the moment, dancing as their uncle plays music for them. Once we begin to be aware of what activities call forth concentration and happiness, we will see many instances in our own lives and in the lives of our children.

In the next chapter we will see several examples of *flow*, mindfulness, concentration, in what we call the *work* of the children.

WORK AS MINDFULNESS

What is *work*? For years I have tried to explain why we in the Montessori field refer to activities that many would consider *play* as *work* in this way. Usually I say something like, "People often think that what a young child is doing is just playing; it is not important; it can be interrupted. But we call a child's activity *work* when he has chosen it carefully and it is something positive that aids his development, and ideally he is deeply concentrating. When we respect this and do not interrupt him, the child develops a positive attitude toward both the work and himself."

When we understand this we often see what a child is doing at home is really his work. We see that many things a child is doing, such as an infant watching a mobile or looking intently at a person's face, a child getting dressed, washing hands, putting objects in some kind of order, building with blocks, drawing, and so on, can have developmental value. It can provide opportunity for concentration, solving problems, and improving mental and physical skills. If we observe carefully we realize these activities are not just something to do as quickly as possible to get it over with, which is often the adult concept of work.

As we have seen in the chapter on *flow*, almost any of our own practical activities in the home, from washing the dishes, to folding laundry, to reading a book, can be seen as something to get over quickly, or something to do mindfully and to enjoy. Even though as adults we still must think of time and efficiency of work in our busy lives, when we give a task to a child we want there to be as many logical sequential steps as possible because this gives much more opportunity for concentration and improves the brain in many ways that current scientific research is corroborating.

It can be frustrating to watch a young child put on his jacket and take it off and put it on again and take it off and repeat these steps over and over. Or ask to be asked to repeat the reading of a book—with no changes— over and over and over. This is not the adult's method of getting dressed or reading a book. But this child is not thinking as an adult, he is working on important things, mentally and physically, and the best thing the adult can do is to give him time whenever possible to respect and protect his *work*.

Here is a favorite quote by Dr. Montessori on *work*:

Does Nature make a difference between work and play or occupation and rest? Watch the unending activity of the flowing stream or the growing tree. See the breakers of the ocean, the unceasing movements of the earth, the planets, the sun and the stars. All creation is life, movement, and work. What about our hearts, our lungs, our bloodstream which work continuously from birth till death? Have they asked for some rest? Not even

We were helping our son move into an apartment and we had not brought anything for his sister's young

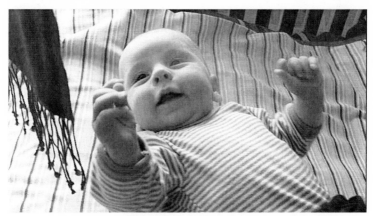

son to work on, so I hung my long red wool scarf from a floor lamp just within his reach. When he first saw it his eyes lit up. He smiled and moved his whole body in anticipation for what possibilities might lie ahead in his reacting with this object. He was not yet at the stage where he could intentionally grasp and release an object, or even reach and touch an object consistently, but his instinct to develop these skills was clear. It seemed that he was using every bit of energy of his whole body to try to touch the scarf. Is this a meaningless activity? No, this is work.

In Bhutan very few children have toys so they are always involved with the work of the family all day every day. They do not do this for praise or attention and certainly not for a reward; it is a natural, daily part of life. A few years ago I was interviewing parents and grandparents in a farmhouse near Paro, Bhutan and we were watching the children as we talked. After a glass of water was spilled on the floor, the elder sister went to the kitchen for a cloth to wipe it up. When she returned, the younger sister reached for the cloth and it was handed it to her. She began to clean up the spilled water. When she was asked to "look at the camera" because I was filming her, she said: "No, I will not look at the camera". It was clear that she was completely involved with her important work and did not want to be interrupted, that she thought her work was more important than having her picture taken.

Noticing how much her little sister was enjoying this, the older sister helped to prolong her enjoyment. She went into the kitchen and came back with a bowl of water. As she sprinkled the water on different areas of the floor the younger sister followed along for quite some time to clean it up.

Two years later I returned. As I come into the farmhouse the little girl ran into the kitchen, got a glass of water, returned to the living room and poured it on the floor. Then after a few minutes she turned to her grandmother and said, in Dzongka, the language of Bhutan, "Why is Susan not taking my picture?" We all enjoyed that.

Later, when we were leaving the farmhouse I saw that these two sisters were lighting a candle from the fire under the water-heating barrel to bring into the house as it began to grow dark. It was clear that being involved continually with the work of the family gave the young girl a lot of opportunity to be focused, to concentrate, to be helpful, and to develop many specific physical and mental skills.

> *Toys and games have their place of course in our Western culture, but having only toys to play with is a waste of energy that could be spent in more valuable occupations. In places like Bhutan where children are included from birth on in the daily life of those around them, there are definitely some advantages. Children are given toys with which they can play, but which create illusions and afford no real and productive contact with reality. Toys furnish a child with an environment that has no particular goal and, as a consequence, they cannot provide it with any real mental concentration but only illusions. They can stir up a child's activity like a puff of air that rouses a tiny flame concealed beneath the ashes of a fire. But the flame is soon spent and the toy is soon thrown away. And yet toys are the only outlets that adults have found for a child's voluntary activity.*
> —**Montessori,** *The Secret of Childhood*

This is a picture from an AMI Montessori Infant Community in San Francisco, California. As in many Montessori environments, preparing food, setting the table, eating with good manners, washing dishes, etc., are important opportunities for physical, mental, social, emotional development of the child. And happiness? It is evident on the child's face; he is happy to be doing something important.

But children are not given a job, even setting a table, until they are prepared. The teacher is adept at analyzing just what skills are necessary to succeed when she gives specific lessons to a child. In order to successfully set the table, the child will have already learned to walk and carry things mindfully, to place an object carefully on a surface, to be aware of which of her friends are present on a specific day so their place should be set, and so on. A lesson should be just at the level to challenge the child to practice and develop a skill but not so difficult that he would be frustrated and give up. This is true at all ages in Montessori environments from birth through high school

Here is an example of adjusting the challenge to the child from one of my elementary, 6-12, classes. A new child joined the class from the primary class. I watched carefully to see what work attracted her and one day saw that she was especially interested in the lesson on the formation of sedimentary rock as soil was washed down a river. So I asked if she would like to record this lesson in her journal. This journal is a place where a student records very special things that he wants to keep forever.

A child usually works on a writing journal entry, or on the second journal that is for mathematical subjects, for a long time, drawing and writing carefully, sometimes decorating the margins with colored pencil designs. In our family we have two sets of these two journals (one for math and one for all other subjects expressed in writing and art) from two of our children and I have shared them many times over the years.

This student decided that in order to show the different layers that settled over the years she would make a key to illustrate a layer of black rock, a layer of red rock, and a layer of orange rock. She worked a long time on this, writing and painting the three colors on the key and the layers.

This was the first time I had seen her writing. As you can see she did some lower case writing in cursive, and then a mix of capital and lower case letters in print. It was clear that I needed to back up and fill in the gaps to prepare her to write beautifully. It does no good to ask a child to write when he wants and needs lessons on *how* to write. This is like asking a child to play a piece on the piano without teaching the body posture, order of the notes, which fingers to use, the timing, etc. Each time the child plays the piece incorrectly the message to the brain is that this is the way it should be played and it becomes long-term memory of that piece of music. And it will be difficult for that child to ever play the piece of music beautifully. It is the same with writing.

Here is a piece of writing from a child visiting from a Montessori class where he was required to write in a journal every day. It is clear that he was writing in cursive but because he was required to write so much he never had the opportunity to back up, slow down, and

learn to write in a way that he enjoyed, where he could concentrate deeply and be proud of his work. In case you cannot read it this is what he wrote (his spelling):

> I hate riting fast and slopily
> I hate riting
> I hate riting
> I hate riting

I hate riting
I love carrots.
I hate riting
Sloppily
Sloppily
Sloppily

In my Montessori elementary training we learned several ways to help children improve their writing. Margaret Stephenson told us that if a child is writing in a messy way we could introduce a new alphabet (maybe

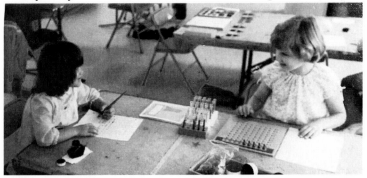

italic if he has been writing in cursive, or the reverse, or cursive if he has been writing in print); we could give him special ink pens with different nib widths (sometimes we made these pens from feathers we found) and different colored inks.

Show him how to carefully write one line of "a's" for example and then examine each one carefully from top to bottom, judging his own details of attempts to write this letter, the slant of the letter, the width of the loop, the way each letter touches or does not touch the line on the paper, and so on, and then to circle the letter that he feels is best.

Give him then a short piece of poetry written in beautiful handwriting to copy.

This is "teaching by teaching, not by correcting." It is adjusting the challenge of beautiful writing to the needs of the child. It gives work that inspires work and concentration. On the previous page we see the girl (on the left) who wrote about sedimentary rock, learning to write with pen and ink.

Here is another student in the class doing the same. As he learns to write beautifully he is also decorating his writing with carefully drawn pictures that he colors in with watercolor paints.

The following is a picture of a piece of work from this class. The author of the story had very bad writing that he did not like, but after a few weeks of the kind of learning-to-write work I have just described he wrote this story in cursive. He wrote it out twice, once in his journal and once mounted on cardboard to take home and frame!

Here is his story. Notice that when he made an error he just calmly crossed it out without getting upset as that is our practice, no erasers in class:

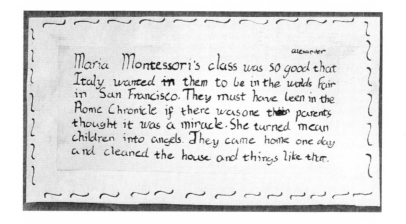

Maria Montessori's class was so good that Italy wanted them to be in the world fair in San Francisco. They must have been in the Rome Chronicle if there was one their parents thought it was a miracle. She turned mean children into angels. They came home one day and cleaned the house and things like that.

Gardening is real work, a way to meet the child's physical, mental, and emotional needs while contributing to the needs of the family. But it is important for parents and teachers to match the gardening work with the child's interests and abilities.

There are many stages in gardening from gathering the tools, carrying them correctly, handling plants carefully as they are placed in the ground, digging the potatoes in such a way that they are not cut, and so on.

Be prepared for children to find practical life work connected with gardening that you might never have thought of. If your child has been in a Montessori class he is probably used to caring for the environment and will have sometimes looked around the classroom for a dirty spot on a window to be glass polished, some dusty

material, a chair that needs washing, or a wet spot on floor — because he wants to do real work.

You might find your child asking to scrub a bucket that you have never cleaned, or to scrape old dried mud off of the shovel. Years ago I went to a workshop given by an AMI teacher trainer on nature and gardening, One of the ideas she gave us was to have a wire brush hanging within reach to scrub out the cement bird bath. I think of her every time I clean our birdbath at home. We have a small round scrub brush and a bucket easily available for anything our grandchildren see needs to be washed.

And of course you might have to think about rearranging your gardening tool area because "a place for everything and everything in its place" is a guiding principle for children because they have such a strong sense of order. Putting away the gardening equipment, rolling up the garden hose, hanging up the shovel, these things are among the favorite gardening activities and provide ample opportunity for work as mindful concentration. In gardening, as in all work, the putting away of the materials is not only to keep the area clean, but it helps the child develop habits of neatness in the environment that leads to orderliness of mind.

At the elementary or 6-12 level, I have found that some children, just as some adults, need absolute silence in order to concentrate and others can do their work uninterrupted by noise in the environment. So in each class I designated two workspaces–one where silence was mandatory and the other where talking was allowed, a work space for each kind of child.

It was interesting, since the children decided what they needed, and each year the sizes of these two spaces were different sizes depending on the children. This child is doing his work in a quiet area, on a terrace outside the main classroom. Everyone knew that he needed silence.

In one environment, it was possible to leave the

classroom to practice guitar, to be able to focus.

It is well known that children at the 6-12 stage of development are more in need of working in groups. Younger children like to have others near by but for the most part they want to work on their own. But children at any age, and adults, are silent when they are creating with deep concentration.

I remember a funny story about this. My teacher trainer, Miss Stephenson, was visiting an elementary class. It was one of those classes where children, almost all of the children, are talking all of the time. After some time she couldn't take it any longer and she stood up from the chair where she had been observing in the middle of the room and called out, "Be quiet!"

Yes it is true that at this age children want to learn to work in groups. The main five "great lessons" are

offered at the beginning of the year to anyone who wants to come, and other small groups, if requested by the students, form spontaneously. But the main work, just as all work for adults and children, is done in a situation where one can focus and concentrate and advance in understanding and skill. This is where the real work occurs.

The girls in this picture are holding a typical planning meeting–dividing up their different roles and responsibilities and work for a group project. After the meeting they went on to find the space to concentrate on their individual research and work. As is usual they had several other such meetings during the implementation of the project and at the end they presented it to the rest of the class at a time they themselves arranged.

It is clear in this picture that some children can concentrate and focus on their work, even with a lot going on around them.

The Evolution Timeline on the floor is introduced at

the beginning of the 6-12 class cycle. But it forms the basis for much of the later work. This picture shows three of the older children, ages 11-13, who have been made aware of a new scientific discovery about early life on the planet and they are examining, quite excitedly, how and where it fits on the timeline. This is not interrupting the work of the two other students in the picture.

In the AMI Montessori teacher training, students spend many hours practicing giving lessons to other adults with a teacher trainer present to answer any questions. In this way the steps of the lesson, the logic of the order of the work, becomes refined, and the ability to give a lesson to a child is stored not only in a book, or in our minds, but in our hands.

Then the teacher can focus on the development of each child in the class knowing just when to give what lesson. She does not have to refer to a book because she is ready to teach.

This explains the success of Montessori, for when the correct challenge is offered to the child he will be able to concentrate on the work, to succeed, to learn.

In the Tibetan refugee Montessori classes in India where I was honored to do a bit of work with the teachers years ago I found that they were very good at this kind of teaching. They were able to give lessons slowly with exact details of movement, keeping the attention of the child who was receiving the lesson, and inspiring the child's own work in such a mindful and careful way. In this picture we see the serious expression on the child's face as he concentrates on building the pink tower as carefully and perfectly as was done in his lesson. And the child next to him is just as entranced as he watches.

Mindful concentration is supported in the work of the child, but for us adults it can also occur if we are aware of the opportunities.

As I was preparing to give the presentation on *Montessori and Mindfulness* on which this book is based in Prague in July, 2017, a young woman came to me ahead of time and said, "I am from India, a Hindu, and I should be meditating every day but I don't' seem to be able to find the time because I have so much to do cleaning the house and washing the dishes and so on."

I replied, "What are you thinking about when you are washing the dishes."

She looked at me with some surprise but before I could even explain I could see that she knew where I was going with this conversation. I said, "When I am reminding myself to wash dishes mindfully I think about each step of the dish washing. It brings me back to the present and I enjoy the work."

She replied with a big smile, "Yes I understand. I will do that!"

MINDFUL WALKING

A few months ago I was walking on a trail not far from our home in Northern California. It was a beautiful day. Suddenly I realized that I was wasting this experience because all I was thinking about was what I had to do when I got home, and what I could have done better the day before and who knows what else. My gaze was down, focused on the path in front of me and my brain was in charge of the day.

For some reason just then I decided to mindfully walk as the Vietnamese monk Thich Nhat Hanh teaches. I thought to myself as I slowed down and paid attention to what I was doing, "Now I am placing my left foot. Now I am placing my right foot." Each step made me more aware of where I was, what day it was, what I was doing.

Almost instantly I heard sounds of birds and the wind in the trees that I had not been aware of just a few seconds earlier, I could smell the dampness of the moss of the forest, and within a few moments of walking like this I detected the sounds of the ocean waves lapping against the shore.

I turned to the left following the sounds and a beautiful vista of the Pacific Ocean, sea stacks, beach,

and the village of Trinidad opened up in front of me. This is what I would have missed had I gone on thinking about the past and the future instead of appreciating the present moment. Being mindful brought together my mind and body.

Paying attention to walking and doing so with concentration and purpose is typical of children when they are young. Children will find a ledge of bricks, or a long piece of board, or in this case the cement edging of a path to our local library, and place one foot after the other very carefully staying on the line.

This innate drive is something that is used in Montessori 3-6 classes to help children with physical development and practice in concentration.

Dr. Montessori did not invent *walking on the line*. She observed it. In 3-6 classes we use the lessons of walking on the line as an example of "teaching by teaching instead of correcting". Rather than telling children not to run in the class we give him challenges to master walking carefully.

In the beginning a child just placing both the heel and the toe of his foot on the line can be challenging enough and can take a lot of concentration. When this is mastered we can suggest further difficulties such as lining up the inside of each foot along the line, or walking with the heel of one foot almost touching the toe of the last one placed.

And as these skills are mastered we give further challenges such as walking so carefully that a small pillow placed on the head doesn't fall off. We can offer the challenge of holding a bell and walking so that it

doesn't ring, or holding a candle and walking so slowly that wax does not drip onto the floor.

In this picture a girl is slowly and carefully walking on the line with a pillow on her head in this Montessori class. Many other activities are going on at the same time as we can see and there are sounds that might be distracting for one not so completely focused and concentrating on walking.

The classroom challenges of walking carefully can depend on the culture. For example one day I was observing a class in London, England where a hot lunch was served each day. Wide soup bowls were used. Each child took the amount that he desired, carefully ladling the very hot soup into the bowl and then carrying it to his place at the lunch table. I saw that one of the exercises on walking on the line in this class was to fill the same kind of lunch bowl with water and then carry it carefully while walking on the line trying not to spill a drop.

These are very practical uses of the line, but there is more. When walking on the line is presented to just one child at a time, as is all other work in the class, and children are free to walk on the line at any time, then it

becomes a walking meditation. I have often seen a child in my own class pause from a particularly challenge piece of work and walk for a bit on the line and then return to his work refreshed.

Here is a personal story of being surprised at the value of mindful walking. This is a picture of my grandson Tai gardening during one of his visits to us in California. When he was four year old I was visiting the family in Portland, Oregon. Because Tai and his sister were getting ready for school and I didn't want to interrupt the morning routine I sat in the living room and meditated. Tai came to me and asked what I was doing and I told him I was meditating.

He asked, "Can I do that?"

I replied, "Children can meditate while walking" and I offered to show him how. He wanted to try it so I said, "Just think about your feet as they touch the floor. When you are putting your right foot down, think 'Right foot.' And when you are putting your left foot down think, 'Left foot'". For a few steps we walked together and then I returned to my seated meditation.

Tai slowly walked away from me and out of the living room, slowly walked through the dining room, then through the kitchen, then through the front hall and back to the living room. He stood silently in front of me smiling.

"How do you feel?" I asked.

His reply? "I am not angry anymore."

This was a surprise. No one knew he was angry. I don't think he knew that he was angry. But after this short period of mindful walking he apparently calmed down and felt happier than he had been before. It seemed that when he became aware of the emotion he stopped being angry.

Walking has been important to many people over the years for many reasons. When visiting Bhutan I was amazed to find that people thought nothing of walking 3-4 hours to get from one village to another for no reason other than to visit a friend. It made me wonder what they were thinking about, was this experience mostly mindful walking?

Einstein's daily walk was sacred to him. While he was working at Princeton University, New Jersey, he'd walk the mile and a half journey there and back. He followed the practice of other walkers, including Darwin who went for three 45-minute walks every day. These walks were not just for health. We know today that there is a lot of evidence that walking can boost memory, creativity and problem solving.

When you think about it, doesn't it make a lot of sense? Walking, like dancing which is highly valued for both children and adults by neuroscientist Adele Diamond, distracts the brain from more cerebral tasks, and forces it to focus on what the body is doing — during walking that means placing one foot in front of the other and not falling over — during dancing a lot more!

A scientific explanation might be that during walking part of the brain becomes quiet and possibly that the part of the brain responsible for processing information, consolidating experiences, solving

problems, or having unexpected insights might be activated.

The Vietnamese Buddhist monk Thich Nhat Hanh, former professor at Princeton and Colombia, nominated by Martin Luther King for the Nobel Peace Prize, is a life long and constant champion of mindfulness, peace and happiness. He has led groups throughout the world in the experience of walking meditation, walking mindfulness. He says,

> *The practice of mindful walking is a profound and pleasurable way to deepen our connection with our body and the earth. We breathe, take a mindful step, and come back to our true home.*

MUSIC AS MINDFULNESS

O ne of my personal favorite ways to be in in the moment with my mind clear of everything else is to be working on a piece of piano music. Music is just one more way to experience flow.

This young child was resting on his mother's lap when someone turned on the radio and music began.

The child immediately turned his head toward the CD player and kept looking in that directions until the music stopped. The mother, who was a Montessori student and later a Montessori teacher, realized what was happening. She did not move but waited until he was through listening.

Even from before birth, human beings are listening. Songs sung to a child during pregnancy can calm him during a stressful period of the day or night after birth. Infants are as tuned in to music as they are to language, and they are aware of every sound in the environment.

In the 1970's I taught in Lima, Peru. Recently I returned to give lectures and stayed with old friends from long ago.

Matteo is the youngest member of the family. The first day in the home of my friends in Lima I played the piano and Matteo sat on his mother's lap and listened. The second day he sat on my lap as I played. At one point he put his hands on my hands and kept them there as I played. We can see the intense focus on his face as he realizes that the sounds he is hearing have something to do with the way my hands are moving over the piano keys.

On the third day again he sat on my lap as I played and he watched carefully. Again he put his hands on mine as I played. Then he pulled my hands off of the keys and played the piano himself. In a few seconds he grasped my hands and put them back on the piano and I played and he watched. Again he pulled my hands off of the keys and played the piano. He did this many times and the family were delighted to see what he was doing, carrying out a kind of research!

After I returned home I received the message that now, whenever Matteo is carried through the living room, he leans toward the piano wanting to play. And, inspired by Matteo's interest, his older sister and brother are taking piano lessons.

Here is another example of a child playing the piano according to his stage of development.

This child has heard other members of the family playing the piano and singing and he is doing the same thing. To our ears the notes he is playing have no relationship to the song he is singing, *Baa, Baa Black Sheep*. But by the serious expression on his face it is clear that he thinks he is accompanying himself on piano as he sings, just as the rest of us do.

This girl is reading music and playing the song on

the Montessori bells in a Montessori 3-6 class in Moscow, Russia. There is a lot of movement and many different sounds in the classroom as children go on with their work, moving furniture, carrying puzzle maps, walking from here to there. But she is entirely focused and unaware of all of this.

As we heard in the chapter on flow, a group as well as an individual can have this experience of everyone working together on the same goal, and concentrating. In this picture, we see an example of this same level of focus in a group of children in Mongolia.

The two girls on the left are playing the *yoochin*, a hammered dulcimer, using two bamboo hammers. The other girl is playing the *chudraga*, a plucked three string instrument. The two boys in the front are playing the famous *morin khuur*, the national instrument of Mongolia. The sound is like a violin or cello, but with just 2 strings. The end of the neck has the form of a horse-head, as Mongolia is a country of people who love horses. It is said to represent the movement and sounds of a horse.

Every Mongolian family strives to have a *morin khuur* in their ger even though they are hand-made and fairly expensive instruments. These children are following the cultural tradition of group flow in their country.

Here is another example of music chosen by the child, and mastered for its own sake. Pia was in my 6-13 class in the US Virgin Islands. She was 11 years old and had never had a piano in her home. In this class, the children had become so independent in their work that I often had time to practice a piece I was learning, *Chopin's Waltz Opus 64 #2*. Pia said she wanted to learn to play it.

When a child asks to learn something in a Montessori class we never say, "No, you are not ready for that." even if we know that it is way beyond his present skill level. We say, "Yes, you will be able to do

... but first you will need to learn this. Are you ready to begin?" And we lead the child to the step he is ready for.

So I showed Pia the symbols on the first measure of the music, and gave her a plastic-covered guide to further symbols used in writing music. I sat with her through the first few measures and told her to come to me whenever she needed help. I was still practicing this piece in order to play it in a wedding in Washington, D.C. at the end of the year, so she was exposed to the whole piece as she worked on it measure by measure.

Pia had her work list for the week and her personal plan for accomplishing it. Each day she finished that work quickly in order to get to the piano. This is a long piece of music and eventually the other students got tired of hearing it. So Pia began coming early to school and staying late to practice, sometimes eating her lunch quickly to practice in the middle of the day. By the end of the year she could play it almost as well as I could and she had it memorized.

In Montessori work the adult is often called a *guide* instead of a *teacher*. This is because the information does not pass from the teacher to the child (as in group lessons) but from the child's actions on the environment, from concentration on the child's own self-chosen work.

The adult functions more like a guide, offering choices, giving 1:1 lessons, and making suggestions for how to accomplish required work when the child is older. So from the very early years students surpass the adult's knowledge, which is wonderful as we can learn along with them.

These students accomplish a level of academic work that is not bound by the level of the knowledge of the teacher. Just as Pia surpassed my ability in playing this Chopin piece by memory (I still cannot) even though I took piano lessons from age 5 and she was just beginning, with uninterrupted concentration and being left alone to think and to work mindfully, there is no limit to what our children can do.

MINDFUL EXPLORATION

Exploration is a strong need in humans varying according to the age and stage of development.

An infant is engaged in exploring his environment visually during all of his waking hours. Notice that, in this example, the child is focused and mindful; he is learning to move his head back and forth

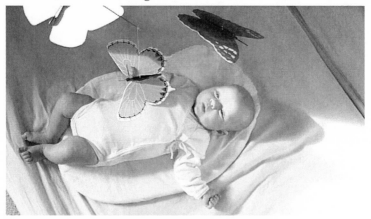

tracking the movement, and looking at the various butterflies in the mobile. His hands are reaching out, an impulse that is preparing him for the next stage of development, reaching and touching those things previously experienced with eyes only.

Working in Morocco in 2015, I visited an orphanage in Casablanca where there was an interest in Montessori because of a local AMI school, but there were no trained people or materials.

Children under the age of one spent most of the day lying on a slanted mattress in a crib because there were not enough staff to sufficiently burp the babies after being fed. When they were a little older the infants spent some time in swings and walkers — objects that we in the Montessori field know not to use.

After thinking about everything I saw, I suggested to the owner of the Montessori school, who wanted to do something to help the orphanage, that they develop a First Year Montessori Project. In the first year of life a lot of vital developmental support can be provided with little training and materials, compared to age one and older.

Over the next year teachers at Ecole Montessori Casablanca volunteered to visit the orphanage, to make

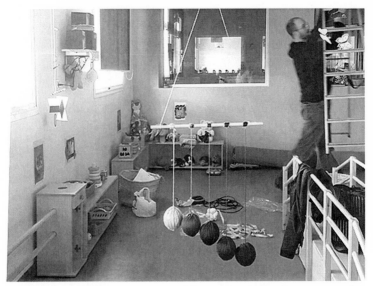

materials, and to create a Montessori environment for the first year.

Two A to I teachers from California who came to the school to consult also volunteered their expertise to help this project.

When I returned to Morocco the following year the changes at the orphanage were dramatic. I met with the staff and the pediatrician connected with the orphanage to share more about Montessori and to hear their stories. They had had no idea that children this young could move, explore the environment, exhibit curiosity, and concentrate as they had now seen. Nor had they imagined that there could be this level of independence.

I heard this comment:

"Their eyes are different. It is as though their eyes are open for the first time."

I have thought a lot about this, wondering what is going on in the mind of an infant who does not have the possibility to move and explore. Where are they and what they are thinking as they stare into space, before their eyes are opened like these children? What is going on in the mind of an infant who wakes up from a nap swaddled and in a dark room, unable to explore with his eyes or move his body? This is sadly a common situation even in the wealthy countries today.

Here is just one story of these new children told by the pediatrician. They had almost given up on one child, the child in this picture, who they thought would never

be able  to move
on his own. He
would only lie
on his back
and rock back
and forth.

But he surprised everyone. After being put on the floor and watching the other children and how they moved about the room, he made his way all the way across the room to climb up on the Montessori "stair" in this picture. It was considered a miracle.

Not all exploration of the young child is valuable; for example if a child wants to see what it sounds like to play a piano with a hammer, or to drop all of the glasses to see if they break.

This reminds me of the old story of someone visiting the first casa dei bambini in Rome and asking a child, "I understand that you are allowed to do what you want." And the child replied, "We don't get to do everything we want but we like what we do."

It is up to the trained adult to assess the situation and decide the value of a child's exploration. In a Montessori class the teacher gives a lesson and then invites the child to do it, and to repeat it as many times

as he likes.

Sometimes the child exactly imitates what she has shown, the example in this picture would be to look for the correctly shaped hole for the different shaped blocks. But sometimes the child explores in another direction and it is still valuable.

In this case rather than doing what we expected the child is concentrating on carefully putting all of the blocks in the bag and then taking them out and putting them on the table and then repeating, and repeating, finally pointing out that there are no blocks left in the bag and smilingly says, "Empty." He has used the exploration to understand and to abstract the concept.

My granddaughter often shows me around her 3-6 classroom when we visit. As we explored the room together, each time she came to something that had not

been put back as well as she thought it should have been, she fixed it, in this case lining up the edge of the red rods that are used to learn the concept of length. Another time she fixed the pink tower. This told me that the teacher was paying attention to the child's need at this age for order, order of how things are done, order of where and how the materials in the classroom are kept, and so on.

It was only because almost everything in the classroom was already kept in good order and neatly on the shelves that my granddaughter could feel satisfied exploring the whole classroom with me and perfecting the placement of those few things that she could correct.

She is completely in the moment and being mindful in this work.

Even at an early age, during the absorbent mind period when the child, with no effort, takes in and learns from everything and everyone in the environment, young children are preparing for the Montessori work of exploring the whole world.

This two-year-old has, with help, put together a puzzle map of the world. He is exploring what he can do with his hands but also exploring language. In this picture he is pointing to the various colors and images, asking for the names, already learning about names of continents and oceans.

At the elementary, 6-12, level and beyond, the exploration is not only motor-sensorial but exploration with the mind. At this age a person begins to be able to

reach out into the solar system and the universe and beyond and back in the far past and recent past, and as a result he will be able to reach with his mind into the future and start to ask questions, draw conclusions, and to make plans. But in order to be mindful and make real progress at this level, the child must be inspired to explore in his unique direction, to have freedom to follow his interests, to set his own goals, and to work toward them.

In this picture we see some of the materials for the first great lesson in the 6-12 class, the creation of the universe, the solar system, and the relationship of the sun and the earth.

The structure of work at this level is not the traditional curriculum that is set by educators, but it is an interwoven exploration based on the five great lessons. These lessons are great stories that introduce:

1 – The Birth of the Universe (physical sciences)

2 – Evolution of Life on Earth (biological sciences)

3 – The Arrival of Humans on earth (studies of humanity)

4 – The History and Development of Language

5 – The History and Development of Geometry and Math

I believe that the main materials that support this Montessori foundation and exploration should always be in plain view, a constant reminder of this structure and inspiring children to explore.

We should not walk into a classroom for ages 6-12 and see mostly books and journals and computers, but timelines on the walls, science and biology experiments, charts to inspire exploration in all areas, a rich and interesting environment. I love it when I am working as a consultant for a school when I can walk into the 6-12 classroom and identify the areas, the materials, for children to explore within and beyond these areas.

This exposure and exploration of the whole of knowledge continues throughout Montessori middle school and high school. Each child follows his own path to the fine details of exploration, but he shares this grand cosmic vision with his classmates.

Because of the vision of the whole that has been presented to him . . . interest spreads to all for all are linked and have their place in the universe on which his mind is centered.
— **Montessori,** *To Educate the Human Potential*

The second great lesson is internalized caring for plants and animals, managing a garden and in this case in a Montessori school in Hawaii making and screening compost, a mindful, challenging, group work. It also provides valuable experience in the fresh air, in nature, and the life lessons that come from close contact with plants, growing and caring for them in such a way that they thrive.

As children are for the most part directing their own

research, there must be a place for them to keep their projects so they can be kept focused on them.

These students will see so many exciting things being explored all around them that they will sometimes experience "runaway exploration" by starting more projects that they can keep track of without a little help in learning to be organized, and a place to keep the experiments, models, art work, and so forth.

Part of the excitement of teaching at this level is that, unlike traditional school where the teacher knows as she enters the classroom in the morning what she is going to do and what the children are going to learn, the

Montessori elementary teacher really has no idea what will have transpired by the end of the day.

She can suggest and invite, but the children decide and we never know what they will do next. As a teacher at this level I found this thrilling, keeping me in the moment and learning new things along with the students.

Here is a picture of an older student returning to the evolution timeline she was introduced to when she first joined the 6-12 class. Children in the whole age range continually return to the basic materials as their research takes them further and further, deeper and deeper, into a subject.

Having the 5 Great Lessons always visible helps them keep focused on the whole range of knowledge instead of being lost in the details. Each time a student returns to an early piece of material such as this timeline, he discovers more pieces of the puzzle of the creation and interaction between elements of our world–leading them to reflect on their own place and potential.

This child is learning about the pictographs of the Egyptians. For this 4th Great Lesson I always kept a chart of the alphabets on display to remind children to keep this lesson in mind as they decided what to study next. The exploration of language is wide and deep, tracing through the imagination how humans first might have needed and begun to use language, which parts of speech they might have needed first, how they might have communicated with strangers, how language changed and spread through the history of migrations and trade.

The teacher watches for interest in this area as in all others and is the facilitator for the student moving forward.

All subject studies—science, biology, the study of humans, art, music, language, the exploration of algebra, geometry, and math—begin in the 3-6 class or earlier. In this picture we see a child in a 3-6 class constructing the *decanomial* or the *square of Pythagoras* just by matching colors and the length of sides of the square and rectangular figures. This child is being prepared to understand subjects that he will later explore in the abstract.

125

These two girls in an AMI school in England, having learned about geometry, algebra, and math with sensorial materials in the primary such as the cube of the binomial, the cube of the trinomial and the decanomial, have set a task for themselves that took them two full days. They decided to square the alphabet. So instead of having a+b or a+b+c, or the ten letters of the decanomial, they will have 26 letters forming the giant square -- a+b+c+d+e+f+g . . . and so on.

On the next page is a detail of their work.

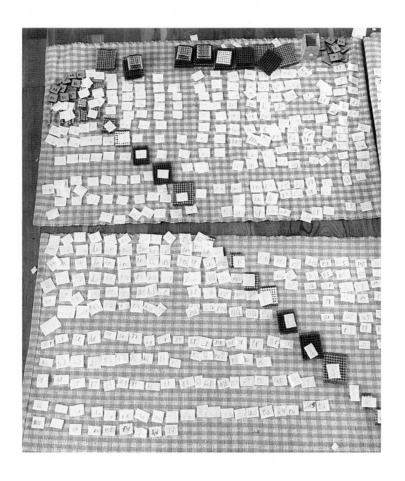

There is a saying:

> *The Teacher is in charge of the minimum,*
> *the child the maximum.*

This means that we should be careful to limit anything that will get in the way of the three-hour work period and the child's own choice of what to work on. If we schedule, teach, or assign work, we will destroy the potential of the child to really enjoy learning and work hard, to reach a high level of concentration.

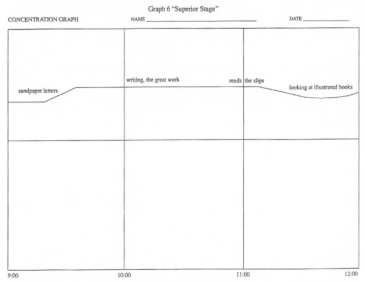

Again let's think about the 3-hour concentration period of the child in this chart.

If, at the 6-12 level, instead of supporting this kind of child-directed exploration and the resulting concentration and mindfulness, we were to fill up the student's days with assignments and schedules, we would never see him tackle such things as learning a Chopin Waltz on the piano, or squaring the alphabet, and so much more.

We would never see the kind of concentration and mindfulness that prepares children to continue to deeply and thoroughly explore the knowing the world, themselves, and how to create a happy and successful life.

As Dr. Montessori said in support of independence and freedom of choice in the elementary class:

> *The mental needs of the child require freedom of exploration, and learning tasks should NEVER be dictated.*
> —**Montessori,** *To Educate the Human Potential*

BORN TO BE GOOD

We have seen that a good Montessori class provides several hours a day of mindfulness for both the adults and the children. And that this kind of mindful concentration brings out the best of one and shows that the goodness, the generosity, the tendency to care for others is a natural human tendency. This tendency just needs help in providing the kind of surroundings that reveals and nurtures it and gives opportunities, depending on the stage of development, for these instincts to become real actions. But that is not always the case.

In many countries where I work, even though the religion is one of kindness and compassion toward others, it is still thought that corporal punishment is the only way to teach children to be good and violence toward children is accepted as normal.

The teacher in this picture, in Thailand, was very kind to the students and it was clear that they cared about him. But when I asked about the stick on his desk

he didn't hesitate to show me and explain that it was the way they train the children to be good.

Once when I was working in Bhutan in the Himalayas, I heard that there was a Montessori school in a monastery in the hills outside of the capital Thimphu. It was not easy to find but my hostess and I persevered.

Finally we arrived and the head of the small two-class Montessori school was very pleased to show us the first classroom. It was a small room in an old building typical of Bhutan country schools. There was a row of desks where children were seated. On the desks were papers and pencils. The teacher was writing something on the blackboard in front of the room and the children were copying it. They looked a bit bored, but happy.

There was no sign of anything at all resembling Montessori materials. As we stood in the doorway watching the class it was clear that the head of school was extremely proud of what we were seeing.

It was difficult for me to phrase a question to find out what was Montessori about this school without hurting his feelings. Finally I asked something like, "What is the most valuable element of Montessori that you are using?"

He replied, with an expression on his face that made it clear the answer was obvious, "In our school we do not hit the children!"

Of course! Somehow he had formulated the essence of Montessori, that children are naturally good, that they do not need to be punished in order to become so.

In 1987 a small group of scientists met with the Dalai Lama. All were involved with some aspect of research studying the mind, and most had an interest in Buddhism because of the many years of experience in this field studying happiness, empathy, and other

aspects of the mind.

Since that time there have been many such meetings; they are organized by the Mind and Life Organization (www.mindandlife.org).

In 2010 six of us Montessori teachers attended a smaller version of these Mind and Life meetings, in Sikkim.

Sikkim is a small country, now part of India, between Nepal and Bhutan. The government of Sikkim had decided to allot 20% of the national budget to education because there were more and more problems as the children of Sikkim came into contact with the modern world through the media. Disrespect, materialism, and violence were becoming rampant.

In their wisdom they had gathered not only educators, but philosophers, Western and Eastern traditional doctors, teachers, psychologists, Tibetan scholars, neuroscientists, and the Dalai Lama, to discuss how to help their children bridge the gap between the old and new world, and to be able to succeed and be happy in their lives.

We were invited because neuroscientist Adele Diamond had given a presentation at a Mind and Life meeting in Dharamsala, India, and was invited to speak in Sikkim. It was her suggestion to include Montessorians. AMI teacher trainers Lynne Lawrence and Jean Miller gave presentations, and four others including myself served as observers. There were 40 speakers and 80 of us observers/commenters at this historic event. You can read more about this meeting here: http://susanart.net/sikkim2010.html

Lynne Lawrence and Jean Miller both spoke eloquently. The Dalai Lama listened carefully and the leaders of the meeting, struck by their words, asked all of us to stay on for another day to continue the discussion of Montessori. I remember one person asking how we handle discipline. To many it seemed inconceivable that children could be good without being punished, that they could be kind, or that they could concentrate and work hard without being manipulated with rewards or threats of punishment. And that they could really enjoy and be happy in school.

One of the many interesting speakers at the Mind and Life meetings, including our meeting in Sikkim, is Dr. Richard Davidson who I have mentioned before. This is what he says about the brain:

Happiness, like any skill, requires practice and

time but because one knows that the brain is built to change in response to mental training, it is possible to train a mind to be happy.

Helping others is not praised in a Montessori environment. It is not rewarded. It is expected and accepted as natural human behavior. In fact we have learned that praise and rewards can destroy the pleasure a child may feel in doing something just to be helpful.

Here is a 2-year-old in a Montessori IC, or infant community, in Japan helping a 1-year-old get dressed in order to go outside.

In Montessori schools we intentionally give children many opportunities to be helpful to others. For example children learn to avoid stepping on a floor mat that marks the space where a friend is working; and they carefully put materials they have been working on back on the shelf in perfect order to be ready for use by a classmate. Even these two seemingly inconsequential examples give practice in caring for others, and elevate a child's self-image and level of happiness. These are true social acts and among the first for very young children.

In this picture a big brother stands still and waits patiently because his little sister offers to help him put on

a cooking apron. He doesn't need help but he knows that she wants to practice tying a bow. So who is helping whom in this situation?

The *practical life* area of the Montessori curriculum at any age includes caring for oneself and the environment and also *grace and courtesy*. This area of work gives children as many opportunities as possible to express their natural caring and consideration for others.

> *If you want others to be happy, practice compassion.*
> *If you want to be happy, practice compassion.*
> —**The Dalai Lama**

Right intention is a very good thing, but right action is maybe better. We have seen evidence that periods of mindful concentration can result in an impulse to be helpful, but where does that impulse go if there have been no examples for children to do good? Of course the adult is the most important first influence in modeling behavior. In face I must say that everyone in my family says "please" and "thank you" many, many times a day just because we are so used to modeling this for young children, grandchildren, and students. It makes a very pleasant atmosphere in the home.

When my youngest child had friends over to play we sometimes played what came to be known as "the popcorn game" and it became a neighborhood favorite. I would fix a very large bowl of popcorn (sprinkled with brewer's yeast as is common where I live) and then 3-5 of us would sit around the bowl and get ready to practice our manners, everyone with a large grin on their faces.

Someone would begin, "Argenta, would you care for some popcorn?"

Argenta, "Yes, I would love some, thank you very much" (as she scooped some popcorn from the large bowl into her smaller one).

"You are very welcome," said the volunteer host or hostess.

Then someone else would chime in, "This popcorn is delicious, and can I serve you some Michael?"

"Yes, thank you very much. You are so kind." Says Michael.

"You are very welcome, I do hope you enjoy it."

And so on.

There is no official end to this game, but everyone had fun doing it, and one year I was voted the most polite mother in the neighborhood!

It reminds me of one question I have been asked by parents often about what to do when their child never says *thank you*. My first question to the parent is, "Do you remind him to say thank you?" Almost always the parent with the problem says, "Yes".

Then I can explain that the child is probably used to being reminded and waiting for the reminder. I can also then explain about the Montessori saying, "Teach by teaching, not by correcting." And we can discuss other ways to teach good manners in an enjoyable way rather than correcting.

One day I was observing in an infant community and I watched a 2.5 year old girl put her work away, roll up a mat and put it away, and then breathe a happy sigh of satisfaction, look around the classroom, and go from table to table tucking the chairs in carefully and quietly (a lesson she had received from the teacher) and then straighten up materials on the shelves. This was her way of expressing goodness and being helpful after a period of concentration.

We also teach children how to get the attention of someone when they are busy. This is different depending on the culture and we teach the appropriate way in a child's culture. For example in my home if I approached two people talking to each other and I had something important to say to one I would stand back a few feet and wait. If they didn't see me I might subtly move so that I was a bit more in the eyesight of the person I needed to speak to. If this didn't work I would probably decide that whatever they were talking about was too important to interrupt and I would go away.

Greetings are taught also depending on the culture. In Peru when I taught there years ago it was polite to kiss a person on the left cheek and then the right, even if you had never met the person before. I remember going to a party, kissing everyone, staying a short time, kissing everyone again, and leaving. In Japan this would never happen, but there is a proper way to bow when greeting a person. In Thailand one holds ones' hands together as in prayer in a "wei" and there are definite understandings about how high the hands should be held depending on the age and "importance" of the person you are meeting.

Handing an object to another person in some places must be done with both hands, and when giving something to a monk in Thailand one places the object on a table and the monk picks it up.

These last few examples have to do with respect for another person, another person's body. In our Montessori classes we teach children to ask permission before touching another person's body. A fellow Montessori teacher once told me that one of her young students had come up to her with a sad look on her face and said, "_____ hit me and didn't ask my permission!"

And just recently after a struggle in our home I watched my grandson say to his sister, asking permission, "Would you like a hug." She replied, "Yes" and the struggle was over.

Cleaning, cooking, putting things away carefully, handing something to another person, offering to help (but only with permission), offering suggestions and advice (but only with permission), hugging someone (but only with permission)—these are all ways that children who have been given these grace and courtesy lessons can act on the good impulses that follow deep concentration.

In my first 6-12 class, after training at this level, I had brought a large, hardcover, etiquette book by Emily Post into class. This book covered everything from where to place the silverware and glasses when setting the table, to how to address a letter to Royalty. At first it was seen as a curiosity of historical interest, but I noticed more and more how much time the older children spent with this book with quite serious expressions on their

faces, and how their manners improved.

Later, consulting in an elementary class in Moscow I was asked how to bring more practical life work, real helpful work, into the class at this level. On that day the classroom assistant was beginning to clean the storage shelves, and two boxes had arrived, each containing a chair that needed to be assembled after class. I suggested that the teacher and assistant take a careful look at everything they themselves do during the day and turn over everything that could be done by a child to the children. The next day a student was organizing the storage shelves much more completely and carefully than an adult might have done, and two students had the metal parts of the new chairs spread out on floor mats and were following the directions to assemble them.

Then I shared with the teacher one of my most popular practical life activities over the years, for any age. It is called "cleaning one shelf." The very young child will do a very simple version. Take a floor mat and place it on the floor next to the shelf to be cleaned. Remove everything from the shelf and place each item on the floor mat in exactly the same way as it belongs on the shelf. Go get a dust cloth. Dust the shelf, bottom, top, sides, back. Put the dust cloth in the laundry basket, and place each item back on the shelf.

This might be followed by washing the dust cloth, hanging it up to dry, drying and putting the cloth-washing materials back in order, replacing the cloth-washing apron, noticing that there are other cloths hanging up that are ready to be ironed, then iron and fold them and put them away. A very *flow* morning.

An older child might do this exercise in more detail, for example more carefully inspecting the shelf to see if it is clean, clean it, and wash or polish all of the items from that shelf before putting them away. Always children seem to be aware that they are helping others.

The young child might have chosen something he has already worked with but often it is a shelf of items for older children that look interesting to him. In this way the child gets to explore the whole room and he feels that he is "giving" to the older children in the class who are usually the ones giving to the younger.

It is also a way for a child to get to touch and explore things used by the older children, and I notice that a child who does this work regularly is much more observant of all of the work being done in the class.

It is so easy to think of more practical life ways for children to be a help to the community once we start noticing how important it is for the children.

Here are some examples for older children.

In the Shree Mangal Dvip boarding school in Kathmandu, Nepal, there are around 300 children who come from far away villages where there are no schools, electricity, post office, or hospitals, and when one asks, "How far away is your home village?" the answer is usually something like, "2 days bus and 8 days walk."

I was asked to spend a week with the children in their classes for their whole day and then come up with ways that they could use Montessori ideas. Of course they have little, if anything, to pay for tuition and the

school does not have money to hire many staff, so the children do much of the practical work.

One of the first things I shared was that their students being required to help with the cooking, cleaning, serving, assisting the visiting doctors and volunteer dental clinics, and to care for each other, was the goal of Montessori education.

I observed an older child checking the cleanliness of the hands of the younger students' hands before they go in to dinner.

From this positive beginning I could go on to talk about the Montessori value placed on real work and caring for one another, and how this is an excellent preparation for life, including their academic work.

After hearing of my work in the Himalayas, a school administrator at an AMI school in Connecticut asked if

there were a way for their elementary students to reach out and help. I visited the school and gave a presentation on the Tibetan Children's Villages in India, the school in Nepal, and Montessori being introduced in Bhutan. They chose to help the school in Bhutan.

During my next trip I sent these students daily pictures and emails that they used to make posters to hang on the walls of the school (which taught me a lesson on the value of proofing before sending!)

They researched Bhutan, studying the food, the clothing, the traditions, and gathering artifacts. Then they held a weekend fair for the whole school community and the public and raised money for the Bhutan school.

As in many places it is not possible to send donations through the mail. Either the boxes do not make it or there is such a high import tax that the school cannot afford to collect the boxes.

the Economics *of* Happiness

So I carried a few things such as sandpaper letters, and cash to have things made in Bhutan. I had brought the names of the students in Connecticut who had organized the fundraiser and left Bhutan hand-carrying a pen-pal letter from the Bhutanese students to each student at the USA school.

A few years ago I shared with elementary students the videos *Ancient Futures* and *The Economics of Happiness*. These are two documentaries that have inspired a grass roots movement to be part of the solution to today's environmental and social problems.

Here is a review from greenplanetfilms.org:

*How can we learn about ecological solutions
from an ancient culture? For more than a thousand
years, Ladakh has been home to a thriving culture.
Traditions of frugality and cooperation, coupled with
an intimate and location-specific knowledge of the
environment, enabled the Ladakhis not only to
survive, but to prosper. Then came development.
Centuries of ecological balance and social harmony
are under threat from modernization. The breakdown
of Ladakh's culture and environment forces us to re-
examine what we really mean by progress–not only
in the developing parts of the world, but in the
industrialized world as well. The story of Ladakh
teaches us about the root causes of environmental,
social and psychological problems, and provides
valuable guidelines for our own future.*

And here is a quote about the second movie by Alice
Waters who trained as a Montessori teacher at my alma
mater in London. She is part of a great movement to
connect children with nature through growing food:

*The Economics of Happiness" delivers a
powerful message about globalization: it is the small,
local economics around the world that are preserving
traditions, cultures, and communities, and
ultimately safeguarding our happiness.*

After they had watched these two movies I asked the students what they thought and I found this feedback particularly interesting, perhaps to be expected from a person who had attended Montessori from age two through to middle school:

> *Kids our age usually think there is nothing we can do to be helpful but this video gives us a lot of ideas and since in the future the world is ours we might as well start now! If we think about it no one can be truly happy when there is a lot of suffering in the world. Many times people hear about all the suffering that is going on but we think there is nothing we can do so we just push that information aside.*
>
> *But inside, somewhere inside, there is a little voice that tells me that the suffering of others prevents me from being truly happy myself. Now I understand that there are things I can do to help and then I don't have to hide the truth from myself. I can listen to that voice inside and do what I can do every day to help. Then I can be really happy.*

I have seen a tendency, as people react to world events today, to believe that we are actors in a play for which the end has already been decided. There is a tendency to hope that experts, all of whom are honest, altruistic, and in touch with each other in order to write that last scene, are handling the problems.

But it becomes clear in the Montessori academic studies that we all have a role to play, and the end has not been decided. In the 6-12 curriculum and beyond, academics are not separated from what is going on in the real world. The broad view of the creation of the universe and the history of life on earth, plants, animals, and humans, prepares students to have a wise perspective, a chance of understanding why things are the way they are, and a path to find their own way to contribute.

These students are very aware that there is past and a future but that it is only in the moment, in the present, where changes can be made.

> *No matter what we touch, an atom, or a cell, we cannot explain it without knowledge of the wide universe. What better answer can be given to those seekers for knowledge? It becomes doubtful whether even the universe will suffice. How did it come into being? How will it end? A greater curiosity arises, which can never be satiated; so will last through a lifetime. The laws governing the universe can be made interesting and wonderful to the child, more interesting even than things in themselves, and he begins to ask: What am I? What is the task of man in this wonderful universe? Do we merely live here for ourselves, or is there something more for us to do? Why do we struggle and fight? What is good and evil? Where will it all end?*
> —Montessori, *To Educate the Human Potential*

Our grandchildren are raised in a family with Jewish, Christian, atheist, agnostic, and Buddhist influences. The result? They have a deep respect for the beliefs of all people, as do all of the family members for each other. They have received the best of all of these belief systems and the areas they have in common, kindness, caring, and respect for all living things and the earth.

In our home we often light incense and fill 7 water bowls. This act has many interpretations but in my practice it gives me a chance to be in the moment and to think of 7 people, groups, situations, to wish the best for. Our grandchildren have participated as soon as they were able to pour water into the bowls. This may look like a ritual but it is really an active concentrated awareness, just pouring water in the beginning. And at

this young age it is a way of improving skills, participating in the life of the family, and giving to others.

Now she is older and doing more than just pouring the water. She can light the candle and the incense and then she stands with the filled bowl in her hands and thinks for a moment, "Now, who most needs my help?"

On our property there is a group of redwood trees. When we stand in the middle, all sounds from outside are muted, and at certain times of the day the sun sends shafts of light in all directions making us feel like we are in a place of worship. We call it the cathedral grove.

One year I was remarking on this as I stood in the center with our two oldest grandchildren. In one voice they said, "We should pray!" and they sat down and prayed for all of the trees of the world.

A few years ago I was getting ready to leave a

school in Tokyo where I was consulting. It was necessary for me to walk to a bus station and take a bus to the airport to leave the city. I was spending the last morning in the Middle School class. One of the students asked if I had a reservation for the bus. I hadn't known this was necessary. So he called the station, handed the phone to another student who was fluent in Japanese, and then the students huddled around a laptop and made the reservation for me. The teacher was not involved. The bus I had been planning to take was full so they found an earlier one. Realizing that I had to leave immediately in order to catch that airport bus, the students handled my luggage, walked me to the bus stop, helped me buy the ticket and we said goodbye. This was a natural part of their day, nothing special.

These same middle school students have the opportunity each day to walk the Infant Community (age 1-3) children from their room down the road to the garden gate, sometimes they read to them, and during emergency drills they are there to comfort them, and the school is always on the lookout for ways for students at all ages to be truly helpful. I think we would call this

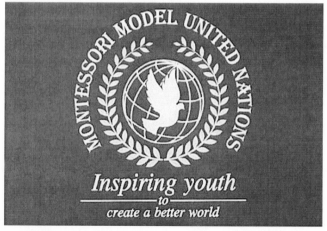

Montessori Middle School practical life, courtesy, and goodness.

In 2013 I gave the keynote address at the Montessori Model United Nations meeting in New York. Here students have a very real experience in being good, being useful. They spend six months learning about a country in the world and preparing to represent a particular country in solving the current problems. Then they attend a two-day global education simulation experience at the United Nations.

When I was there the new president of Malawi had heard about this and contacted the director on the first day to inform her that she was very willing to listen to and consider whatever suggestions the students had for solving the problems of Malawi.

Here is an example of a grown up Montessori student, our son Michael, experiencing such an opportunity during one of his two trips to India, first as a student, and then as an environmental volunteer in India:

> *This morning two friends and I went to the Mother Teresa Orphanage and spent a couple of hours. All the kids there are the ones that no parents will adopt because they have some kind of physical or mental defect. A lot of the kids had Polio and couldn't walk, and one little girl was only about 1 foot tall and had a very deformed face, she had no arms only hands growing out of her sides. We spent a lot of time with her because I think that no one really plays with her because of all her imperfections.*
> *There was another boy who had very weak legs so we spent a while moving his legs for him and*

trying to get him to exercise them. Eventually he began to straighten and bend at the knee and then he got very happy and started laughing when I touched his feet and moved his toes. None of the women who ran the place spoke English, and most of the kids were completely mute. We didn't really know what was wrong with some of the kids and we couldn't ask cause we could not communicate with anyone but we managed to help with some things.

This has opened up for me what is important in life and what is not so important. And I know that this feeling might not be with me for very long, but hopefully each time, it sinks in a little deeper and stays with me longer.

Several of the Mind and Life meetings mentioned at the beginning of this chapter have resulted in published books. *Train Your Mind, Change Your Brain* was one of them. Here is a quote from this book review:

Contrary to popular belief, we have the power to

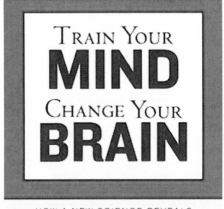

literally change our brains by changing our minds. Recent pioneering experiments in neuroplasticity– the ability of the brain to change in response to experience–reveal that the brain is capable of altering its structure and function, and even of generating new neurons, a power we retain well into old age.

The brain can adapt, heal, renew itself after trauma,
compensate for disabilities, rewire itself to overcome
dyslexia, and break cycles of depression and OCD.
And as scientists are learning from studies
performed on Buddhist monks, it is not only the
outside world that can change the brain, so can the
mind and, in particular, focused attention through
the classic Buddhist practice of mindfulness.

Just as the West has much to teach in the medical and other fields, the East has as much to teach in the area of mindfulness, compassions, meaning of life, and happiness. This book has been quite well received by the Montessori community because it proves that for those who have not had their natural mindfulness protected from birth, it is not too late.

I would like to end this chapter with a quote from a speech Mohandas K. Gandhi gave at the Montessori training center in London in 1931, speaking to Dr. Montessori:

You have very truly remarked that if we are to
reach real peace in this world and if we are to carry
on a real war against war, we shall have to begin
with children and if they will grow up in their
natural innocence, we won't have the struggle, we
won't have to pass fruitless idle resolutions, but we
shall go from love to love and peace to peace, until at

last all the corners of the world are covered with that peace and love for which, consciously or unconsciously, the whole world is hungering.

CONCLUSION

It was suggested by Lynne Lawrence, General Director of AMI, and Sona Havlickova of the Montessori Institute Prague, that I speak on Mindfulness at the 2017 congress. It felt like a research suggestion having been made by a Montessori teacher who knew that I had a passionate interest in the subject, a situation where neither knows what the results of the exploration would be. I am grateful.

Over the 3 months of preparation it seemed that everywhere I turned the word "Mindfulness" was turning up. It seems to me that perhaps because of all of the greed and suffering we hear about daily in the news today there is an even stronger and more unifying movement to dig deep into the goodness of the human being with hope for the future. It reminds me of the saying by Dr. Martin Luther King, Junior:

Only in the darkness can you see the stars.

Although it is clear that carrying out Montessori practice, in our schools and in our homes, is a tested way to bring about the benefits of mindfulness, there are many people living mindfully in many different situations.

Also as a result of this research I have learned to curb my tendency to go out and preach the gospel, but instead to remember the value of my own practice. In his book *The Miracle of Mindfulness*, Thich Nhat Hanh says:

> *In a family, if there is one person who practices mindfulness, the entire will be more mindful. Because of the presence of one member who lives in mindfulness, the entire family is reminded to live in mindfulness. If in one class, one student lives in mindfulness, the entire class is influenced.*

There are many ways to be mindful — observing children, walking, washing dishes, gardening, playing the piano, doing yoga or tai chi, worshiping — I find, after 45+ years of meditation practice, that seated meditation at least once a day and ideally twice, is necessary for me to approach being the kind of person I want to be, and to remember to be mindful in other situations.

It helps to remind myself of advice I gave a parent many years ago about music practice. Our children were students of violins, violas, and piano and we Suzuki parents were learning along with them.

Practicing piano seemed easier because it is there ready to be played but for a stringed instrument it was different. First the student had to open the case and remove the instrument. Then have the tuning checked if he had not learned to do it yet. Then carefully take the bow out of the case and tighten the horsehairs at the base or frog of the bow. Then get out the resin and resin the hairs of the bow. Then get out the shoulder rest and attach it to the instrument. And only then can one begin to practice.

So what I told the parents was that I only "required" that our son practice his violin for one minute. After going through all of the preparation I just described, he always practiced more than 1 minute!

When I think I just don't have time for that second meditation I aim for one minute. I sit down, relax my body, close or lower my eyes, place my hands in a relaxed position, take a couple of deep breaths sometimes watching the inhale and exhale, and notice — not judge but notice — what I am feeling or thinking. I then remain usually for more than one minute, but if not, just doing these few things to prepare to meditate brings me into the present moment calmly.

With a seated meditation I don't need any equipment, nor do I need to be anywhere else. Meditation is not an escape from reality or my daily responsibilities but rather a way to be nourished physically, mentally, spiritually, to be refreshed and ready to get back to more mindful work.

I would like to share with you a slightly simplified version of one of my favorite illustrations by Dr. Montessori from her book The Absorbent Mind. I often show it when I am working with schools.

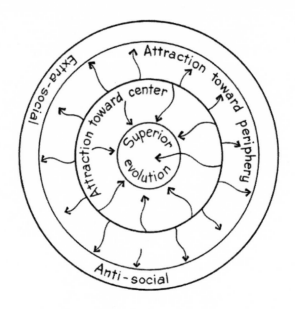

Here is some of her text referring to this diagram:

One of the chief reasons for the spread of our schools has been the visible disappearance of these defects in children as soon as they found themselves in a place where active experience upon their surroundings was permitted, and where free exercise of their powers could nourish their minds. Surrounded by interesting things to do, they could repeat the exercises at will, and went from one spell of concentration to another. Once the children had reached this stage, and could work and focus their minds on something of real interest to them, their

defects disappeared. The disorderly became orderly,
the passive became active, and the troublesome
disturbing child became helpful in the classroom.

I urge you to go to her book and learn more. I often have this picture in my mind and I think of it in a variety of applications. It keeps me focused on the essence, the very core, of our Montessori work. It is a constant reminder of just how far we can go, as parents and teachers, in affecting the life of a child. We can invite, suggest, offer, guide, but we must constantly remind ourselves that it is the child who has the secret of his own development and his own future.

Attraction to the periphery or the outside of this circle could be seen as a person being controlled by others, teachers, society, TV and other media ads that dictate what a person should buy, look like, weigh, wear, earn, believe, drive, and what he should think is the goal of life. Attraction to, and living under this influence, in the periphery, creates a false idea of who one is and just what life is all about. It creates a kind of packaged identity leading to competition, separation, and envy. Certainly not to community, compassion, and happiness.

The inner circle in my mind represents the inner wisdom that is available to all of us through mindfulness. In schools and in other situations where independence and freedom of choice is common, and concentration is protected, children — who are naturally attracted to the center from birth—can continue to dive deep and be in touch with the wisdom that resides there. This is true for us adults as well because this wisdom resides in all of us.

It is my hope that the ideas and experiences I have shared will help in our work with children, and in our own lives. When I was asked to speak on mindfulness I sent an email to Sona to ask if she had anything specific in mind that she was hoping I would talk about. She replied that it was her hope that there would be something, perhaps a tool, that one could use to make us more mindful, to make our own lives better and also the lives of children. So I am going to share just a bit more about daily

mindfulness.

Here are the words of Thich Nhat Hanh from a video clip that I shared:

There are many ways of eating a tangerine. There was a young man to whom I offered three tangerines. And he ate them while talking about his projects.

He peeled a tangerine and threw sections of the tangerine in his mouth and ate unconsciously while thinking only of his exciting projects. I was there, present. I looked at him eating his tangerines.

I thought that, well, I was wasting my tangerine.

He has already eaten two tangerines. There is only one left.

So I said, "Jim, stop. Eat your tangerine."

So he stopped. He is an intelligent person. He stopped talking.

He breathed. He peeled off the tangerine, smelled, slowly, slowly, all his attention taking one section, looked at it, put it in his mouth, felt the juice coming out on his tongue, ate slowly. And then took another section.

And he ate his tangerine in that way.

The tangerine became real.

And the person who eats the tangerine becomes real also.

And after he ate that third one probably I said, "Good."

Because I did not lose that tangerine.

A child in the first year of life is watching carefully everything going on around him. He is concentrating, mindful, learning. Even in the first year of life, if given a spoon or fork, he will imitate his family and concentrate deeply, repeating the movement he has observed in others over and over, for a long time, until he gets it right. Eating is not just for nutrition for this child, but to learn to control his hand, to learn by repeating, to eventually manage to get all of the food actually in the mouth perfectly, to taste it thoroughly, to fail and to try again without help or interruption. This work strengthens his body, his mind, and his spirit.

This is just one example of the human striving to master his world and to improve himself. And potentially, if the parent realizes the importance of this work and has the time, it can occur more than once a day. Can we adults also use eating as an opportunity to be mindful, to be better, happier?

Speaking of both children and adults, Dr. Montessori said:

...hidden in their hearts there is something deep, common to all. All have a tendency, however vague and unconscious, to raise themselves up; they aspire to something spiritual. And this tendency, however slight be its action on the defects of character, exerts sooner or later a pressure towards improvement. Both the individual and society have this in common: a continuous tendency to progress. There is a tiny light in the unconscious of mankind, which guides it towards better things.

—Montessori, *The Absorbent Mind*

Before a child can walk on his own it is possible for him to learn to pull up on a wagon like the one in this picture. He can practice pulling up and sitting down, pulling up and sitting down, according to his own needs, until he has had enough of that work for the day and turns to something else.

Then he learns to push the wagon and move forward strengthening his legs in preparation for walking alone.

In this picture the child has pushed his wagon quite a long way through a field of mustard flowers.

Occasionally he sat down, reached for a flower, examined the color and the texture, sat for a few moments thinking, and then pulled himself up and continued walking. This was his work and no one offered unnecessary help, nor did they interrupt.

But when through exceptional circumstances work is the result of an inner, instinctive impulse, then even in the adult it assumes a wholly different character. Such work is fascinating, irresistible, and it raises man above deviations and inner conflicts. Such is the work of the inventor or discoverer, the heroic efforts of the explorer, or the compositions of the artist, that is to say, the work of men gifted with such an extraordinary power as to enable them to rediscover the instinct of their species in the patterns of their own individuality. This instinct is then a fountain that bursts through the hard outer crust and rises, through a profound urge, to fall, as refreshing rain, on arid humanity. It is through this urge that the true progress of civilization takes place.
— **Montessori,** *The Secret of Childhood*

May our own journeys to discover the best of humans and protect it in hopes of a peaceful future on earth, be joyful and full of wisdom, and may they succeed.

Montessori Research by Angeline Lillard

D r. Angeline Lillard, professor of psychology at the University of Virginia, Montessori student and parent, student of the AMI Assistants to Infancy course, author of *The Science behind the Genius*, and my friend, also spoke at the AMI Montessori Congress in Prague in 2017. I am grateful to her for permission to share her 2011 article on Mindfulness practices in Montessori schools.

For the sake of readability the references and research have been removed. Most of the remaining quotes are from Dr. Montessori and when she quotes "Hanh" she refers to the Vietnamese monk referred to elsewhere in this book, Thich Nhat Hanh.

171

You can find the entire article and credits at her website. Also there you will find research she has conducted on the success of Montessori depending on the materials that are used in the environment, for example her paper, "What belongs in a Primary Classroom."

Her website: http://www.montessori-science.org/

MINDFULNESS PRACTICES IN EDUCATION: MONTESSORI'S APPROACH

Montessori schooling is a 100-year-old system that naturally incorporates practices that align with mindfulness and are suited to very young children. Here I describe how several aspects of Montessori education, including privileging concentrated attention, attending to sensory experience, and engaging in practical work, parallel mindfulness practices. These aspects might be responsible for some of the socio-emotional and executive function benefits that have been associated with Montessori education, and they could be adapted to conventional classroom methods.

Recent years have seen an increase in research incorporating mindfulness practices in education with the aim of improving children's well-being. Mindfulness is a quality of focused attention on the present moment accompanied by a non-judgmental stance; its systematic cultivation has been called the heart of Buddhist meditation although it need not be accompanied by subscription to Buddhism or any other belief system.

Mindfulness interventions with adults are clearly related to well being; by contrast, lack of attention on the present, or mind-wandering, is associated with less happiness.

While bringing standard yoga and meditation practices to high schools and even middle schools appears to have positive outcomes for students, research with very young children is in the early stages and is challenged by the issue of age-appropriate practices. For example, one successful pilot clinical intervention with anxious 7- to 8-year-old children found that 3–5 minutes of sitting focusing on the breath was age-appropriate. How long might be appropriate for preschoolers? Interestingly, in Tibetan monasteries in the north of India, formal meditation training does not begin until ages 17 or 18.

One place to look for approaches to helping even younger children to be mindful is Montessori education. Montessori education includes many practices and values whose goals and structures are consistent with mindfulness. Montessori education was initiated over 100 years ago by Maria Montessori, one of the first women physicians in Italy. Dr. Montessori used materials stressing sensory discrimination to improve the cognitive achievements of children with mental retardation, which led to development of a full activity-based educational program for children from birth through age 12; development of the adolescent program was ongoing when she died in 1952. Although Montessori education has very positive impacts on school achievement, it is fundamentally aimed at the development of the whole person. Its emphasis on deep concentration, integration of mind with body, practical work, and specific exercises like "The Silence" and "Walking on the Line" all echo mindfulness practices. These as well as other points of similarity in mindfulness and Montessori practices and values are discussed below, followed by a discussion of parallel outcomes.

Deep Concentration

In both Montessori education and mindfulness practice, concentrated attention is central. In Buddhist practice, meditation is a means to mindfulness. One meditates by focusing one's thoughts on a single idea or experience like the breath, and this builds the capacity for focused attention. Although trained by meditation, concentrated attention is not confined to meditation but is to be applied throughout life, to listening and to eating, to every act and movement. Hanh recommends that, "When you eat an orange, [you] try to practice concentration" because "Joy and happiness are born of concentration".

Concentration is also highly valued in the Montessori classroom. Dr. Montessori believed concentration led to a psychologically healthy state she called "normalization" — a term she borrowed from Anthropology that essentially meant "being a contributing member of society" but which also meant that children were constructive and kind in their behavior. Further, she believed that this state is the most important outcome of focused work. Dr. Montessori described the event that brought her to this realization: a child was so deeply engrossed in her work (placing ten graduated cylinders in their correct holes) that her chair was lifted up in the air, and the other children (at Dr. Montessori's direction, as an experiment) danced and sang around her without breaking her concentration. Once children have begun to concentrate on work, according to Dr. Montessori, they become "completely transformed ... calmer, more intelligent, and more expansive," bringing out "extraordinary spiritual qualities". "After this phenomenon of concentration the children are really 'new' children. It is as though a connection has been made with an inner power...and this brings about the construction of the personality. Children who have come to concentrate are said to behave better, no longer "prey to all their little naughtinesses".

To support the development of deep and sustained concentration, Montessori education has 3-hour work periods during which a child can pursue a single line of self-focused work. The goal is full absorption. In contrast, conventional schooling is typically organized around shorter periods of work focusing on the external stimulus of the teacher. For example, in elementary school, there might be a 40-min math lesson when the teacher stands at the board, first going over the previous night's homework then instructing children in a new math procedure. In kindergarten classrooms, activities might change every 10–15 min. Attention spans and the ability to control one's attention increase with age as the prefrontal cortex develops. Attention is trainable in children, and certain school experiences might serve to provide such training.

Having longer work periods focused on interesting, absorbing work is consistent with the mindfulness practice of training the attention, and observation of good Montessori classrooms suggests that when the work is absorbing, challenging, and self-directed, young children do engage in deep and sustained concentration for long periods.

Grounding the Mind in Sensorimotor Experience

Mindfulness training involves particular attention to sensory experience. One mindfulness exercise, for example, is to fully experience eating a raisin or some other food, considering its texture and shape and color, how it feels in the mouth, how it tastes on different receptors on various parts of the tongue, and so on. Attention to all sensory experiences — the sounds of birds, the feeling of one's chair, the color of a flower — is emphasized. Attention to motor movement, from focusing on how one walks in walking meditation to body flexibility in yoga to one's movements in activities of daily life, is also prominent. The sensory and motor systems connect the mind and the body, taking sensory information in from the environment and executing motor acts that change one's position in the environment and the environment itself. Thus when one attends closely to sensory and motor experiences, one integrates body and mind. Hanh writes, "Our motto is: Body and mind together."

Montessori education begins with grounding in sensory experience via motor movement. Three-year-old children learn to make fine distinctions between different smells, sounds, tastes, colors, textures, and so on, manually pairing those whose sensory qualities match. For example, primary (3- to 6-year-old children) classrooms contain sets of musical bells, eventually used to make music, but initially used to train the ear to distinguish sounds. The teacher will even set the various bells around the room, and the child needs to pair up the ones that match by moving around the classroom, playing each one, carefully attending to its sound and holding that sound in mind while moving to a different bell to play its sound. In addition to establishing sensorial focus, this exercises working memory (attention capacity). Montessori also has tasting and smelling exercises, where a child pairs objects that taste or smell the same, often while the child is blindfolded.

Another Montessori activity that involves attention to sensory and motor experience is "The Silence Game". The teacher chimes a bell and the entire class falls silent and listens, with the aim of becoming fully aware of their surroundings. When the silence is broken, children can discuss what they experienced, in particular, what they heard. Dr. Montessori noted that young children "love silence to an extraordinary degree". "All those who are on a higher spiritual plane [...] have felt a need for silence". In addition, Dr. Montessori noted that once Silence lessons were instituted in classrooms, children became more careful in all their actions, and even "became more kind".

The attention to sensorimotor experience in Montessori education extends to the care Montessori children are asked to take in how they move in and interact with the environment.

The Montessori curriculum includes "Lessons of Grace and Courtesy," in which one attends to one's behaviors and their effects on others. Children are given lessons in how to walk carefully around the room, not stepping on others' workspace, and how to carefully push in a chair so it is straight and even and not in others' way. "Every exercise involving movement where mistakes can be corrected ... is of great assistance to a child... Our children become agile and alert by learning how to walk around various objects without bumping into them". In a good Montessori classroom, children are asked to be mindful of their every action and how it might affect others. "Walking on the line" is a specific Montessori game that resembles walking meditation: the child carefully places one foot in front of the other, exactly on a circular line. Children attend to the feeling of placing the foot and moving their weight from one leg to the other, learning to walk mindfully and in balance. "The attention of the child is centered, concentrated, upon this line... This exercise also shapes the personality".

Children in Montessori classrooms often get their work on trays that must be carried carefully and parallel to the floor or the contents will slip. This requires attention to how the tray looks and feels in one's hands. Once they arrive at their work place, children need to carefully set up their materials as the teacher has shown them to do. Each object has a place and method of use, such as the objects in a Japanese tea ceremony. In addition, children often do their work on rugs, which are kept rolled up in a container in the classroom. When a child wants to work on a rug, he or she takes one out, finds an appropriate place on the floor for it—where there is room, and outside of pedestrian channels—and unrolls it. Then the child walks—not skips or runs, which can disrupt others—and gets the work. The child returns to the rug and sets down the materials, then carefully sets them up and carries out the work. When finished, the child carefully replaces the objects in their correct positions on the tray and returns the tray to the shelf, lining its edge up with the edge of the shelf, and then goes back to roll up the rug. Rugs are to be rolled tightly, with attention to evenness—just as one might carefully roll up the yoga mat. All a child's actions in a Montessori classroom are thus to be carried out with attention to the body and the objects in the environment.

Mindfulness practice incorporates this same level of care regarding movement. For example, Hanh describes an incident from his days as a novice monk, when his teacher asked him to do something and in his excitement he went out the door mindlessly. The teacher called him back, and he knew it was so he could close the door "with 100% of my being... Since that day, I have known how to close the door behind me".

In conventional schools, in contrast, activities highlighting attention to sensory experiences and movements are not typically part of the curriculum, except in "specials" like art, music, and physical education or sports. By first grade, most of the child's school day is spent sitting in chairs listening to the teacher's words. Even if children are in activity-based classrooms, specific attention to how one moves and what one senses, as goals in and of themselves, is not a key part of the typical early school curriculum, which focuses on literacy, math, science, social science, and art. Montessori education includes all these areas, but incorporates movement throughout and gives equal prominence to sensorial education and "Exercises of Practical Life".

The Practical Work of Life

Closely linked to grounding in sensorimotor experience is attention to the functional activities needed to sustain everyday life. A Zen proverb states that one should chop wood and carry water, before and after enlightenment, and Kabat-Zinn suggests that one "attempt to bring moment-to-moment attention to the tasks, experiences, and encounters of ordinary living such as setting the table, eating, washing the dishes, doing the laundry" and so on. An emphasis on finding meaning in everyday activities that sustain life is seen in Montessori education as well, where children from a very young age engage in the "Exercises of Practical Life". A budding toddler can carry his or her food to the table and clean the table after clearing dishes. In the primary classroom, young children become absorbed in scrubbing furniture, polishing shoes and brass, and arranging flowers. Specific organized steps are followed in carrying out each of these activities. The Montessori adolescent programs often include hard work on farms and nature preserves, as part of community service work. Dr. Montessori observed that, "There is a strict relationship between manual labor and deep concentration of the spirit". Practical activities are fundamental in Montessori education, and children can engage in them and see their meaning from a very young age. The child needs "activity concentrated on some task that requires movement of the hands guided by the intellect". Learning to polish a shoe, for example, a child carries out a careful sequence of steps, knowing the goal—the shinier shoe that he or she will really wear—and seeing how each step serves this eventual goal. When society is agriculture-based, probably many more of children's daily activities have this clear connection between an action and a practical, cognized goal to which young children can relate, connecting body and mind.

It is much more difficult for a young child watching an adult typing at a computer to grasp the practical end: the abstractions underlying journal publications, grant submissions, financial spreadsheets, or stock purchases are beyond their intellectual capacities. The activities of practical life in Montessori education are thought especially important, because they provide a functional ("important to my life today") goal to which a child can relate and a series of bodily movements—guided by the mind and attentively engaged with—that the child can use to get there.

Conventional schooling has little of this. Instead, children are steeped in abstract mental pursuits or what is provided as relief from them, a recess, with little attention to how body and mind can work together to pursue practical aims. In most American schools, children do not engage in activities to sustain daily functioning — working in the cafeteria to prepare food or do dishes, sweeping the hall, and so on, although in Asia, such practices are common. Instead, conventionally schooled children are told it is important to listen so they can do well on a test so that they eventually can get a degree that might help them get a job to support themselves — distant goals that lack tangible meaning even for adolescents.

Other Points of Similarity

Three other points of similarity across Montessori education and mindfulness practices are an emphasis on simplicity, an avoidance of judgment, and grounding in stories. An additional interesting intersection lies in the training of Montessori teachers.

Simplicity

In mindfulness practices and Montessori education alike, there is a value on simplicity. Mindfulness practice is fundamentally simple: focus on the breath. Pay attention. Be aware. A meditation retreat is an exercise in simplicity: do yoga, sit, eat, walk, sit, do yoga, sit, eat, sit, and so on. Buddhist texts repeat the same material again and again. Through repetition of simple yet profound exercises, one is expected to reach higher levels of engagement and understanding. Montessori also uses repetition within simple frameworks to bring about higher levels of understanding. The Montessori classroom is uncluttered and pristine, with only as much material as the children need to further their development. "Overabundance debilitates and retards progress". Unused materials are removed or rotated out until there is a need for them. For the most part, there is only one set of material for each type of work—one pink tower composed of ten cubes, one set of 12 metal insets, one binomial cube, one set of material for flower arranging, and so on.

Non-Judgment

To be mindful is to be non-judgmental: one is to notice, but not make good–bad judgments. "Mindfulness is cultivated by assuring the stance of an impartial witness to your own experience. To do this requires that you become aware of the constant stream of judging...and learn to step back from it". Meanwhile, one needs to learn to "trust in your intuition and your own authority". Yet, in conventional schooling, we train children that teachers are the judges and will reinforce their judgments with grades, gold stars, and demerits. A child's own sense of authority is rarely paramount in this setting; rather, they are subjected again and again to adult judgment.

Montessori education avoids extrinsic authority judgments in many ways. First, it uses self-correcting materials. A child who needs to match 20 sensory objects into ten pairs, for example, will typically notice if he or she made an error because she will reach the last two and discover they do not match. When the errors are not noticed, the assumption is that through repetition, children will come to recognize many of their mistakes and self-correct. When that's not the case, the teacher will re-present a material— not by telling a child he or she is wrong, but rather by simply gently re-presenting how to use the material. In these ways, a Montessori child can avoid feeling judged by adults. Learning takes place within the individual through concentrated interaction with interesting materials; the child becomes his or her own authority. Children do continually make judgments as part of the work—which piece of sandpaper is more rough or smooth, for example—but they are not repeatedly subjected to a teacher assigning grades.

Learning from Stories

Another point of similarity between Montessori education and mindfulness is the use of stories. Buddhism is based in tales— monks tend to educate with parables, tales of what happened to the Buddha or in their own lives that can instruct us. Stories are a powerful way for humans to learn, as we tend to represent experiences as narratives. Montessori education, particularly at the elementary level, also bases learning in stories. The underlying structure of the elementary curriculum is actually five great stories: the birth of the universe, the beginning of life on earth, the beginning of humankind, and the invention of symbols and math. At five points in the first few weeks of each school year, the teacher seats all the class in a circle for these stories, and tells one of these stories in dramatic style, replete with props (for example, there is often an explosion in conjunction with the Big Bang in the first story). These core stories are followed by several other narratives associated with five core areas of the curriculum (although the interconnection among the different areas is a key component of Montessori education). Montessori's elementary curriculum is called "cosmic education" and its main underlying point is that everything is interconnected. "To teach details is to bring confusion; to establish the relationship between things is to bring knowledge". For example, the invention of the Pythagorean theorem might be detailed in a story about Pythagoras on vacation going down the Nile, watching the rope stretchers redraw property lines after a flood. This connects math, history, geography, and language.

In Buddhism as well, stories are repeatedly used to help the students understand, and there is also an emphasis on the interconnectedness of all things—the interconnection of life and death, our own interconnections with all people and things.

Dr. Montessori might have been directly influenced by Eastern philosophical traditions when creating the elementary curriculum, since she designed much of the elementary curriculum during her years in India, where she was establishing a training course when WWII broke out. Because she was unable to return to Europe during the war, she had an extended and productive 7-year-stay in India.

Teacher Training

185

As a final point, in Montessori education, teachers are asked to examine their inner selves, reminiscent of mindfulness training. They are to become aware of their own psychological "issues," so they can keep them aside and focus on the child's needs, without allowing their own unsatisfied desires to interfere. "A teacher must prepare himself interiorly by systematically studying himself... A good teacher does not have to be entirely free from faults and weaknesses [but should know what they are]". The attitude Montessori counseled teachers to have toward the children bespeaks "loving-kindness" — a basic precept of mindfulness. "A teacher ... [must be] ready to be there whenever she is called in order to attest to her love and confidence. To be always there — that is the point". In addition to being always there and always loving, Montessori teachers are asked to be very careful observers of children, tuned in and aware of when a given child would be ready for the next lesson. This Dr. Montessori believed was the most fundamental quality of a good teacher.

In order to help Montessori teachers reach a point in their own development when they can serve children in these ways, their training involves an intensive full academic year with a deeply experienced teacher–trainer (at least as implemented by the Association Montessori Internationale which Dr. Montessori founded to carry on her work). These teacher–trainers have spent at least 4 years as apprentice trainers, after at least 5 years as Montessori teachers and at least one in their own training, thus they are themselves very deeply grounded in Montessori education. In my own Montessori teacher training, every morning for 30 min, we lay on the floor in a darkened room and listened to Pachelbel's Canon, while the trainer guided us through a relaxation. In all training courses, the trainer also observes emerging teachers working with children and discusses their interactions. Thus Montessori teachers are expected to be transformed, as people in their training to become teachers, in ways that are akin to the changes brought on by engaging in mindfulness practices.

Do these elements of Montessori schooling translate into outcomes similar to those seen in Mindfulness research? The next section explores some parallels.

Outcomes Research

The research on outcomes of mindfulness practices in adults is burgeoning, and there is a growing literature on the outcomes in children and adolescents. Research on the outcomes of children in Montessori programs is much more limited. Here, I note parallels in the outcomes in two areas (attention and social behavior/knowledge) where they exist, but with an important caveat: noting parallels across the program outcomes does not mean that the outcomes necessarily stem from the same source. Although Montessori education includes practices that bear similarity to mindfulness ones, Montessori education also includes practices that bear no similarity, for example, 3-year age groupings, and allowing children free choice in their activities. These features of the program might be important sources of outcomes. Because Montessori is a whole system, one cannot remove aspects to test the impact of parts. Thus these points of similarity in outcomes are offered speculatively: in mindfulness interventions using randomly assigned groups, we can be fairly sure that it was the mindfulness intervention that caused the change, but with Montessori education outcomes, other aspects of the program could be necessary to the found outcomes.

First I will describe the methods used in the four high-quality studies of Montessori outcomes with which I am familiar. I consider these high quality because (1) they used randomly assigned samples or attempted to match samples, and (2) they used high-quality Montessori programs ("Montessori" is not a trademarked term, and there are many schools that use the label, but do not follow the practices described in her books very closely).

There are four quality Montessori studies whose outcomes parallel those in mindfulness intervention research. Two used an experience sampling method with middle school students who were matched with middle school students from conventional schools. One paper focused on the level of engaged interest, and the other on social relationships and time use in school. A third study compared children at ages 5 and 12, whose parents had entered them in a random lottery to go to a public city Montessori school, when they were 2–3 years of age. Half of the children had been admitted to the Montessori, and the other half was enrolled at other mostly public schools in the district. Children were tested on a variety of social and cognitive outcomes. A fourth study compared 2- to 6-year-old children in classic Montessori classrooms (those following Dr. Montessori's program very strictly) with children in supplemented Montessori and conventional classrooms. Income, ethnicity, and parent education were the same across classrooms, and the conventional schools were ones that Montessori parents most often said they would send their children to in areas where Montessori is not available. A range of social and cognitive outcomes was tested.

Attention

Children randomly assigned to Montessori primary classrooms in which they have 3-h work periods have been shown to have better executive function than children who lost the Montessori lottery and instead went to other schools. In addition, children in classic Montessori classrooms show significantly greater increases in executive function over the course of the school year than do children in conventional or supplemented classrooms. In addition, Montessori middle school students report feeling significantly "greater affect, potency (i.e., feeling energetic), intrinsic motivation, flow experience, and undivided interest (i.e., the combination of intrinsic motivation and high salience or importance)" while doing schoolwork than do matched students in conventional middle schools. These findings of improved attention are paralleled in mindfulness research. Even a short-term course of meditation training improves attention skills; and 3 months of training was sufficient to improve performance on a dichotic listening task and show underlying changes to neural networks involved (Lutz et al. 2009). The attentional networks of long-term meditators are especially efficient. Mindfulness interventions benefit focused attention over and above good control procedures like relaxation training.

Social Outcomes

Mindfulness training programs encourage loving-kindness and empathy, which would seem likely to improve relationships. Intervention studies with medical professionals have shown social relationship benefits including increased empathy, and therapy with non-distressed couples has been shown to improve relationship quality.

Such findings are also paralleled in Montessori research. For example, Montessori middle school children will more likely claim their schoolmates are also their friends as compared with matched controls. In the random lottery-based study, the 12-year-old Montessori students will more likely report trust in their classmates and choose the most positive option in social problem-solving tests. Montessori 5-year-old students will more likely engage in positively shared peer play and less likely engage in ambiguous rough-and-tumble play on the playground, will more likely choose a more advanced form of moral reasoning in a social problem-solving task, and will more likely perform better on theory of mind tasks. The latter two results were also shown in children in more classic Montessori classrooms.

Thus there are parallels in social and attention-related outcomes for participants in Montessori classrooms and participants in mindfulness practices. Whether the parallel outcomes stem from parallels in activities in the two realms is not known.

Summary

Many points of similarity have been discussed here between mindfulness and Montessori education, such that one might even view Montessori education as a form of mindfulness education. In both programs, there is an emphasis on deep concentration as a source of personal development, leading to balance and joy and, by extension, to healthy relationships with other people and the environment. In both, the close connection between body and mind is respected; Montessori's sensorial exercises are a unique educational format in which this connection is emphasized, but the connection runs throughout the curriculum, as the educational program involves hands-on materials in which the body and mind work together to solve interesting problems. The exercises of practical life are also an extension of this and resonate with the call to chop wood and carry water. The self-grounding effects of functional activities are recognized in Montessori and mindfulness. Each encourages attention to the body and its every movement, to executing every act with care and precision. Several other points of similarity were also raised: the use of parables, the value of simplicity, and the absence of judgment. An additional point of interest is the mindfulness inherent in Montessori teacher training programs.

Some educators today are interested in how we can incorporate mindfulness practices in education, and Montessori education offers several ideas to consider. Very young children can and will focus attentively on meaningful work that incorporates body and mind. They also will be mindful of their actions when shown how to be so by attentive and loving adults. As education's goals grow beyond having more children circle more right answers on multiple-choice tests, Montessori education might provide some guidance for an alternative route that can nurture wiser and kinder and also knowledgeable human beings—a far more important goal that is perfectly compatible with doing well on those tests.

One of the most striking findings in studies of the impact of school-based mindfulness programs like sitting meditation and yoga concerned the control groups. For instance, on measures relating to psychological health, across the course of the year, while children in mindfulness programs tended to improve, those in control groups clearly declined. Our conventional schools have a poor person–environment fit, and mindfulness interventions help ameliorate these ill effects.

A LITTLE MONTESSORI HISTORY

Maria Montessori was born in Italy in 1870 and became one of the first female medical doctors in this country. In her work at the University of Rome's psychiatric clinic, Dr. Montessori developed an interest in the treatment of children and for several years wrote and spoke on their behalf.

At age twenty-eight, she became the director of a school for mentally disabled children. After two years under her guidance, these children, who formerly had been considered uneducable, took a school examination along with normal children and passed successfully. Educators called Dr. Montessori a miracle worker.

What was her response? If mentally disabled children could be brought to the level of normal children, what does that say about the education of our normal children? For the rest of her life she conducted research, trained teachers, and continually discovered the secrets of the life of children.

Montessori's says in, *The Absorbent Mind*:

> *In our first schools the children used to enter when three years old. No one could teach them because they were not receptive; yet they offered us amazing revelations of the greatness of the human soul. Ours was a house for children, rather than a*

real school. We had prepared a place for children where a diffused culture could be assimilated from the environment, without any need for direct instruction. The children who came were from the humblest social levels, and their parents were illiterate. Yet these children learned to read and write before they were five, and no one had given them any lessons. If visitors asked them, 'Who taught you to write?' they often answered with astonishment: 'Taught me? No one has taught me!' At that time it seemed miraculous that children of four and a half should be able to write, and that they should have learned without the feeling of having been taught.

The press began to speak of 'culture acquired spontaneously.' Psychologists wondered if these children were somehow different from others, and we ourselves puzzled over it for a long time. Only after repeated experiments did we conclude with certainty that all children are endowed with this capacity to 'absorb' culture. If this be true, we then argued, if culture can be acquired without effort, let us provide the children with other elements of culture. And then we saw them 'absorb' far more than reading and writing: botany, zoology, mathematics, geography, and with the same ease, spontaneously and without getting tired.

And so we discovered that education is not something which the teacher does, but that it is a natural process which develops spontaneously in the human being. It is not acquired by listening to words, but in virtue of experiences in which the child acts on his environment. The teacher's task is not to talk, but to prepare and arrange a series of motives for cultural activity in a special environment made for the child.

If we follow these rules, the child, instead of being a burden, shows himself to us as the greatest and most consoling of nature's wonders! We find ourselves confronted by a being no longer to be thought of as helpless, like a receptive void waiting to be filled with our wisdom; but one whose dignity increases in the measure to which we see in him the builder of our own minds; one guided by his inward teacher, who labours indefatigably in joy and happiness, following a precise timetable, at the work of constructing that greatest marvel of the Universe, the human being.

We teachers can only help the work going on, as servants wait upon a master. We then become witnesses to the development of the human soul; the emergence of the New Man, who will no longer be the victim of events but thanks to his clarity of vision, will become able to direct and to mold the future of mankind.

Early in the movement Dr. Montessori observed the problems with moving too quickly, compromising too much, and so in 1929 created an organization in order to be consistent in standards of teacher training.

This is the AMI or Association Montessori Internationale in Amsterdam. Anyone — parent, teacher at any level, birth educator, university student, homeschooler — is welcome to be a member of AMI.

The mission of Association Montessori Internationale is (from the website):

> to support the natural development of the
> human being from birth to maturity, enabling
> children to become the transforming elements of
> society, leading to a harmonious and peaceful world.

There are AMI affiliate societies in several countries around the world. At the main AMI website you can find a list of all AMI teacher training courses and all affiliate societies. There is also a section called "Aid to Life" which provides information and video clips concerning the development of movement, communication, independence, and self-discipline in the first years of life. The Aid to Life part of the AMI website is being translated into several languages: **https://ami-global.org**

A division of AMI is EsF, or "Educateurs sans Frontières". (From the website):

> EsF builds capacity by connecting Montessori
> teachers, advocates, students, schools

and organizations with communities, social entrepreneurs, local officials and policy makers, to improve the visibility and credibility of Montessori education and consequently increase its availability and access.

Here is a list of some of the EsF initiatives:

At risk and under-served populations – poverty, refugees, prisons

Remote and Indigenous communities

Public education

Initiatives for adolescents

First years of life

Preparation and support for Parenthood

Special needs children

Montessori approaches for the elderly

ABOUT THE AUTHOR

It was November 1963, Bombay, India. I had just turned twenty. The sky was clear blue and the day was calm, my thoughts interrupted only by the sounds of honking horns and the smell of cardamom wafting from a large vat of chai being cooked over an open fire, surrounded by men in long white pants and loose shirts squatting and chatting as they drank their morning tea.

Suddenly everything glittered and I felt as though I were being struck by lightning and lifted up. It was a pleasant sensation that lasted but a split second. The fellow student I was with said that without warning I had just sat down on the pavement, staying there without moving for several minutes staring straight ahead, and he had not been able to reach me. I had no memory of sitting down, no memory of anything beyond the lightning strike.

Life went on, but I was changed. From that moment on I no longer could stand to eat meat and more than anything else I wanted to find out what had happened to me. You can imagine how I enjoyed this quote from *Montessori's Absorbent Mind*, as she spoke of the circle illustrating the center and periphery:

> *We have a difference not unlike that between vegetarians and non-vegetarians. Many eaters of meat abstain from it on certain days of the week. During Lent they fast for forty days, or go with out meat and other luxuries. They find this a really long penance and hold it a virtue to resist the temptation. These are people who keep rules that others have made, or which have been given them by their spiritual directors. But the inner circle would not contain these: it would be a circle for vegetarians, men whom meat does not tempt. These avoid meat. For them no missionary is needed, for they keep the rules wholeheartedly of their inner natures.*

Being a vegetarian was not a choice, and I do not judge others on their food preferences, but it became part of my nature from then on.

Today I am still thinking about what happened that day in Bombay, but from that moment on my life path became clear. Those men were my brothers. Everyone I meet is part of my family. Each experience brings me closer to what I was when I was born, one small unit connected with every other atom and molecule in the vast universe. I now know that this is what I was experiencing on that day in Bombay, when I was "struck by lightening." I do not have a plan but take each moment as it comes, each life lesson beginning at the surface and then settled deep inside, one more piece of the puzzle of life.

Since that day I have earned degrees in philosophy, world religions, education, and three AMI Montessori diplomas. I have studied Sri Aurobindo and Teilhard de Chardin at the Asian Studies Institute in San Francisco, meditation and healing at the Berkeley Psychic Institute, and Tibetan Buddhism at the Library of Tibetan Works and Archives in Dharamsala, India. Books and words and lectures are not lightning, but they are a preparation and an explanation.

I have been baptized Presbyterian and Catholic, had an audience with the Pope, taken refuge as a Tibetan Buddhist, met the Dalai Lama, and danced the Hora with friends when the new Torah arrived in our town. I have worshiped in Saint Peter's in Rome, in mosques in Albania and Morocco, in cathedrals in Lima, Peru, in small temples in Bhutan, and while circling the giant stupa in Nepal. I celebrated my 60th birthday praying for the world on the roof of the Potala in Lhasa, Tibet, and this year Sufi danced in the hot steaming Cauca Valley of Colombia, South America.

The holiness and goodness I have felt in these places is very much like what I feel when I see a child in a Montessori class finish a bit of concentrated work and then walk up to a friend and give him a hug or when a child drops a cup of beads and two or three friends automatically gather to help him pick them up. I can feel it when I watch my children pet the dogs and cats they have rescued, or when my 5-year-old granddaughter explains to me how we must all take care of our rivers. Or sometimes just when I am listening to a piece of music, washing the dishes, or walking on the beach or in the woods.

And each day, as I meditate and sometimes become one with the object of my meditation, even for few seconds, I find myself in that place, no longer separate. Some call it *grace*. Connected, protected, safe. Then I stand up and smile, sometimes laughing, full of strength and aware of what to do next to help the world be a good place.

For more about this work see her website and blog at www.susanart.net

BOOKS IN THIS SERIES

The Joyful Child: Montessori, Global Wisdom for Birth to Three

Susan Stephenson's book truly reflects the spirit and purpose of Montessori in a way that makes the philosophy translatable to both new parents and veteran Montessorians. Susan's passion for the pedagogy, her extensive experience, and her world travels resonate as she explores the universal, emotional, and psychological depths that construct the child's development.

—Virginia McHugh, past Executive Director of The Association Montessori International USA (AMIUSA)

Child of the World: Montessori, Global Education for Age 3-12+

This book explains the meaning of life, how you are supposed to live it. It would be helpful to other people my age. If the young person does not want to read the chapter, The Young Adult, Age 12-18, *then the parents should read it so they can help their son or daughter become a better person.*

—Ryan Alcock, Montessori student, age 13, Amsterdam

Stephenson's volume is a wonderful resource for parents seeking thoughtful, sound advice on raising well-grounded children in a chaotic world. Presenting Montessori principles in clear and eloquent prose, Stephenson's legacy will be a tremendous service to generations of parents to come.

—Angeline Lillard, PhD, professor of psychology, University of Virginia, author of *Montessori, The Science behind the Genius*

The Red Corolla, Montessori Cosmic Education (for age 3-6+)

Susan Mayclin Stephenson, Montessori trained 0-3, 3-6, 6-12, with experience at all levels, writes many practical books about Montessori education. Her book, The Red Corolla: Montessori Cosmic Education, *translated into many languages, has a section titled: The Work of the Child. In this section, she has a sub-section on Physics in which she shares how to do many science experiments. She describes how to set up the science experiments and gives presentations. This book is a wonderful resource for a primary teacher (3-6 year olds) all taken from Susan's primary training in London many years ago. The book also deals with other areas of science, e.g., botany, zoology, plus music, geography, art, history, etc. If 3-6-year-old children can experience as much as possible of these materials, they have created a lovely foundation for the Cosmic Education of the elementary years.*

—Judi Orion, Director of Pedagogy,
Association Montessori International (AMI)

What I like about this book is the possibility that it will give to teachers who have not learned in their training this way of presenting the various cultural areas—art, music, geography, biology, and physics—to young children. That is, how to offer it in such a way that the child freely chooses to absorb the materials. Scattered throughout the book is information on approaching various ages of children, not just the young one.

—Rita Zener, PhD, AMI 3-6 Montessori Teacher Trainer

The Universal Child, Guided by Nature

The Universal Child, *more than anything else I have read, helps me understand the value and potential of a Montessori education.*

—School administrator new to Montessori, USA

Simple, elegant, inspiring. Susan Stephenson carries Dr. Montessori's vision of education for peace forward with this lovely, simple book about what we can all recognize as universal in our make-up as human beings. Those things that ought to (and can) bring us to a place of great respect for children through positive, intelligent engagement with them the world over.

—Gioconda Bellonci, Montessori parent and teacher

Montessori and Mindfulness

The author has a deep and broad understanding of Montessori and life long experience with meditation. Supplemented by wonderful pictures and stories from worldwide travels, this book gives a sound portrayal of how mindfulness manifests in this most profound and wise approach to children's education. Many thanks!

—Angeline Lillard, PhD, Professor of Psychology, University of Virginia, author of *Montessori, The Science behind the Genius*

The author writes with such clarity and simplicity yet takes on the complexity of Montessori philosophy and contemporary thoughts on mindfulness with such grace and care. Her overall theme that personal fulfillment leads to care for others and for our environment echoes throughout each chapter and creates a wonderful symbiosis of Montessori thought and Mindfulness practices, with interestingly retold personal stories throughout. I really like the way Susan distills the essence of Montessori into such an accessible and inspiring book.

—Lynne Breitenstein-Aliberti, Association Montessori Internationale, United States (AMIUSA)

207

No Checkmate, Montessori Chess lessons for Age 3-90+

This book can tell you how to teach chess to any child in a Montessori way. But if you look past the chess, you can use this book as an insight to teach your child anything, using the Montessori method. The book introduces the game of chess using: grace and courtesy of handling the chess pieces, and the social aspect of the game; practical life— polishing/dusting the pieces, setting up the environment; language, using the three-period-lesson to learn the names of the pieces; mastering the game by building up one difficulty at a time. This is the essence of Montessori. If you are not interested in learning chess this book is still a gold mine of knowledge and insight into the Montessori method and how to offer any skill to a child. As always, this author welcomes you into the world of the child and how to help spark their interest.

—Joanne King, Montessori primary and elementary consultant, the Netherlands

If you are looking for a book that will help you to introduce the game of chess to your child—in a non-competitive, gradual, and fun way—you have found it! Deep respect and understanding of human development in its formative stages is a common denominator of all Ms. Stephenson's books. In No Checkmate, *you will find a conceptual framework of developmental characteristics along with a practical guidance in the form of preliminary games and activities, gradual introduction to the key rules of the game, and more. This book opened a new field of exploration and joy for me and my two daughters!*

—Dmitry Ostrovsky, father, philosopher, Montessori elementary teacher, Israel and Russia

Montessori Homeschooling, One Family's Story

I highly recommend this book for Montessori teachers for ages 6-18 even more so because it reminds us that we offer keys to the world and a variety of ways for the child to explore it. As teachers, our vision is to lend an inspiration only until the child's own inspiration is lit and this book shows us how this can be done both through practical glimpses into the family's homeschooling days, as well as through the examples of the homeschooler's own journal reflections.

—Christine First, Montessori adolescent program, New Zealand

Our English department teachers read Montessori Homeschooling, One Family's Story *and then made a presentation to all the Middle and High School staff. The experience of their son was very impressive for the whole group of teachers. When students recognize the purpose and are a fundamental part of what they are learning, they are more likely to dig deeper, and find ways to learn about what is important and relevant to them. Teachers have come to nurture our students' desires and help them connect to their passions and interests.*

—The English teachers, Montessori Colegio Bilingue, Cali, Colombia

The author shares valuable, informative methods for how to teach and interact with children and teens. I am using the author's techniques at work with children from ages 7-18 with great success. Susan shares ways to treat children with respect and dignity and receive that respect in return. Examples of

209

how to achieve reciprocity are abundant in this gem of a book. This is a must-have for parents or people working with children of all ages and backgrounds.

—Kathy Wollenberg, counselor for young adults, USA

Each chapter describes one year of home schooling from kindergarten through twelfth grade. It is encyclopedic in detail and charmed with honesty about failures and successes. This is quite a span, with the right kind of limited stimulus exposed at the right ages and stages and leading to wider independence. It comes through with the widest scope at adolescence. They had four guidelines: keep the developmental stage in mind, prepare the environment and offer the work, observe to see if it is working, and lastly, adapt and "follow the child". This Montessori-inspired home-schooling centered in the family ended with Michael's acceptance at Brown University. It is more than a fairy tale; it is a triumph for all families to witness.

—David Kahn, Director Emeritus of NAMTA, North American Montessori Teachers Association, adolescent education speaker and consultant

Aid to Life, Montessori Beyond the Classroom

Chapters include:
Peru, A Montessori Class without Montessori Materials

A Montessori Q&A Newspaper Column
Nepal, Montessori for Forgotten Himalayan Children
Tibet, Braille without Borders
Tibetan Children's Villages
Montessori Teachers with the Dalai Lama in Sikkim

It was Mr. Montessori's dream that his mother's, Maria Montessori's, educational approach could be realized without being bound to a set of materials. He would be very pleased with this book. The author, Susan Stephenson, is fulfilling her dream in showing how all children can receive the Aid to Life that they need to develop their potential. It is very readable book, full of real life situations. The table of contents intriguing for finding just the answer one is looking for. This book will give confidence to parents who want Montessori for their child beyond the classroom.

—Rita Zener, PhD, AMI Montessori Teacher Trainer

This is a wonderful book about Montessori and how it is being used in many countries. We will be translating it into French.

—Victoria Barres, Association Montessori Internationale representative to UNESCO, The United Nations Educational, Scientific and Cultural Organization. Paris, France

211

Please Help Me Do It Myself, Observation and Recordkeeping for the Montessori Primary and Elementary Class (2022)

Chapters include:

FINAL CHAPTER
Becoming a Young Adult

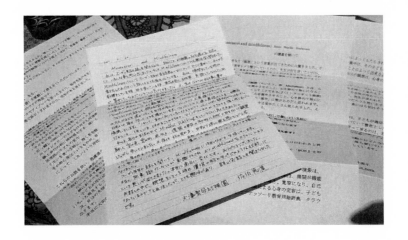

LETTER FROM JAPAN

Aika Watanuki Mariani is a friend and colleague living and teaching in Italy. At the congress in Prague she translated my presentation *Montessori and Mindfulness* to a group of 13 people who had come from Japan. Just before this book was to go to print she notified me that she had received moving letters from these teachers about the presentation.

Thank you Aika for translating the talk and this letter. It is my sincere hope that reading this book will be a help to many as the Prague presentation was.

Dear Susan,
Thank you very much for your lecture on
Mindfulness and Montessori at the International

Montessori Congress in Prague. Your talk made me think a lot about the children in my care. You also made me reflect on my own actions and words.

After your talk my mind was full of questions such as: "How am I as a Montessori teacher?", "How do I practice mindfulness in my everyday life?", "How can I share that precious gift in my classroom?", "What makes a peaceful classroom?", and "Where do I go from here?" (Note: She has been teaching over 15 years.)

You shared with us examples of when you are mostly concentrating during the day. I thought about myself and would like to share my examples with you.

I am very concentrated or "beyond thoughts" when I am cleaning up my house, or when I am cooking or when I am having a lovely walk among nature. I never thought before that I was this focused on these things but I was indeed very much into what I was seeing or doing.

There is a child in my class who has a hard time concentrating on anything. But yesterday, I did walking on the line with him, and observed him carefully. Then I realized one important fact — with every little step he made he was trying to concentrate as much as he could.

I thought about your lecture and the word mindfulness. *How I would like to be able to observe more of mindfulness in my children's actions and* words. And to lead or direct them or let them lead me to see the discovery of the child as Dr. Maria Montessori did.

Ever since I came back to Japan, I started to give myself more time and enjoyment of mindful walking. I feel deeply nurtured by what I learned from your lecture.

Every morning, on my way to school, I see the beautiful sky and I am very thankful. The sky shows us a different color everyday. Also, the shapes of clouds, the wind, little flowers on the street and its colors and shapes, all this is new and blessings for me.

In the evening, I hear the insects crying, so I know the season is changing. Everything in life changes and we are never the same. At night, I gaze at the stars and the moon shines beautifully. This is my home and I want to share its beauty and sense of wonder with my children.

Nature is telling me to slow down. Relax. Breathe. Find a balance between my mind and heart. From the unknown to awareness. I have seen the changes within myself and how I see the world in front of me. I would like to deepen my practice and understanding of mindfulness as I grow.

Thank you again for your inspiration. I look forward to reading your new book in Japanese very soon!

Yours sincerely,

M. S., Fukuoka, Japan

Made in United States
North Haven, CT
28 June 2022

20743065R00136